Outskill

Outskill

Future-Proofing
Your Career in the
Post-Pandemic
World

PARTHA BASU

HARPER
BUSINESS

An Imprint of HarperCollins *Publishers*

First published in India in 2021 by Harper Business
An imprint of HarperCollins *Publishers*
4th Floor, Tower A, Building No 10, DLF Cyber City,
DLF Phase II, Gurugram, Haryana – 122002
www.harpercollins.co.in

2 4 6 8 10 9 7 5 3 1

Copyright © Partha Basu 2022

P-ISBN: 978-93-5629-266-6
E-ISBN: 978-93-5629-267-3

Typeset in 11.5/15 Apollo MT Std
Manipal Technologies Limited, Manipal

Printed and bound at
Thomson Press (India) Ltd

To Pramatha Ranjan Bose, my father,
and Dipika Sinha, my mother-in-law.
I lost two of my favourite people during the time
this book was being created.

I wish you both were here to hold the book. Miss you!

'It is possible to fly without motors,
but not without knowledge and skill.'

—*Wilbur Wright*

Contents

SECTION 3
Future-Proofing

Introduction

When I started writing this book, I was reminded of Charles Darwin's theory of evolution, developed by him in the nineteenth century. I understand that the phrase 'survival of the fittest' was coined by Herbert Spencer after reading Charles Darwin's *The Origin of Species*.

I am not an expert in natural sciences, but when I try and relate this theory to the ever-changing corporate world, we can safely state that professionals who can adapt to changing environments will have more chances to excel in their career versus the rest who are not ready to embrace a change. Survive the change. We need to constantly adapt and evolve to shine, but if we decide to wait and watch, we might perish.

Hence, the theory is applicable to all of us in the corporate world, even 150 years after it was first developed, and it will continue to guide us for years to come.

Before I proceed, let me tell you why I decided to title this book 'Outskill'—

Many of us often hear about the need to unlearn and acquire new knowledge through which we can ensure that our skills are refreshed to fit our changing job requirements. We all go through various trainings; some of us venture into self-learning which entails acquiring new skills. Outskilling is about going beyond regular processes of learning and development, and further widening our horizons. It is about understanding the future need for skills—what your current or future employers might need in the future. Outskilling makes you ready for a new role, be in within the organization or outside it. You embrace the skills that are needed to remain relevant in this rapidly changing world, narrowing the skill gap so you can fit into a variety of organizations.

Many organizations today are actively investing in their employees to make them ready for the next challenge. They want to ensure that their employees are future-ready. I understand that in mid-2019, Amazon announced that they will be investing $700 million to train 1,00,000 workers in new skills. I also read that PricewaterhouseCoopers announced an investment of $3 billion in the digital upskilling of about 2,75,000 people— through training their people and in technologies for supporting clients and communities.

It is our life, it is our career. We are the only losers if we sit back and not do enough to embrace the future. Hence, should we wait for organizations to help us outskill? Why can't we take a few steps ourselves and be ready for the next challenge? What is stopping us from 'becoming' future-ready?

Change is everywhere, be it due to advances in technology, evolving socio-economic scenarios, shifts in demographics, the birth of new sectors or slowdowns in economies. Organizations that did not even exist fifteen years ago are now giant corporations, while on the other hand, long-established brands and organizations have taken a beating. Physical boundaries are disappearing at a faster pace with the advent of technology. Processes are changing, and getting standardized.

It was against this backdrop that the ground beneath our feet shifted almost overnight. The pandemic arrived, pressing pause on existence around the globe, redefining life as we know it. We were unsure what business-as-usual will look like after this is over. But unprecedented global crisis aside, many of the changes we see now were already creeping up on us. COVID-19 may have simply sped up their adoption.

In the past few years, I have come across many articles and books that talk about how the world will change due to fast-evolving technology. Every other day, I read about how many of us will lose our jobs due to such changes in the world; how the activities that are rewarding today will cease to exist over time.

Enough has been written on this subject. This book is not about that.

But when I read those articles and studies, one of the conclusions I came to was that the way we engage and work in the years to come will be very different from how we do so today. Three things leapt out at me:

1. Technology will lead the way.
2. Virtual working will be on the rise.
3. The workforce of tomorrow will be looking for flexibility, purpose and authenticity versus selling time to earn a mere salary.

And then, I asked myself:

1. Do I have the skills required in this changing world?
2. Will I survive in this fast-changing world?

3. Will my team be valued for the skills they have today, or do they need something else?
4. How do we prepare the next generation for a workplace that we haven't even begun to imagine?

And thus the big question is: if the biggest changes are happening, all thanks to technology and the evolving ways of working in a purpose-driven world, what can we do to ensure that we stay relevant in the years to come?

I decided to explore my unanswered questions by speaking to senior leaders in various industries. I spoke to about forty-five leaders and tried to cover varied industries to get a wider view from those who, I believe, are facing these challenges every day, and adapting themselves and guiding their teams to adapt. I wanted to hear from the 'ground'.

Thus, this book is not only the product of my own research and views, but contains the experiences and wisdom of leaders across industries.

The verdict is clear: there is no time to wait. We need to outskill and be ready to fit into the post-pandemic technology-driven world. We need to adapt and learn new skills or else the road ahead will be tough. Panic won't help, rather it is imperative that we deal with our emotions, take stock and equip ourselves to adapt and evolve.

And as I could not find a relevant book on this topic, I created one.

This book will tell you how to inculcate and internalize the qualities you need in the virtual, digital world to help you distinguish yourself as a leader in this changeable yet exciting landscape. There are qualities, skills and habits you can develop to ensure that you remain relevant and effective, no matter what the challenges ahead.

This book is not a recipe to overcome uncertainty in your career. No book can be. But it aims to help you navigate it with greater awareness, lots of preparation and most importantly, by identifying the probable core traits you need to adopt to make yourself earthquake-proof.

While I have endeavoured to cover all relevant points, if you find that I have missed something, please do write to me so I may continue to learn.

I repeat what I wrote in my last book *Mid-career Crisis*: we all grow up hearing stories from our parents and grandparents. Till date, I remember many of those stories fondly. I believe that we don't remember much of the wisdom that management or self-help books shower on us. If we remember something, it is the stories. Thus, all topics that I have covered in this book have a story attached to them.

All of them are 'near' real-life stories—some experienced by me, some by my colleagues and friends, and some told to me. However, in order to protect privacy, I have changed the names and provided a fictional touch to the stories, as required. As you read, you may find many characters familiar to you. If you can relate to them, put a face to them and learn from their experience, I will be happy that my effort to write this book was worth it.

I hope you will find this book interesting and useful.

SECTION 1

What the Future Holds

1

Future Is Technology, Technology Is the Future

We all know that change is coming, and in many ways, has already come. The buzz about artificial intelligence, big data, the internet of things, machine learning and predictive analysis might be relatively new, but information technology has been transforming our world over the past fifty years, and the pace of change is growing. The modern workplace is almost unrecognizable from what it was even ten years ago. Certain jobs and functions have appeared and disappeared in half that time. Others have sustained.

Technology has been one of the top enablers for the change we are experiencing. Some technological advances may affect a particular sector; some have an effect on the entire world. Technology has given us access to data and real-time analysis, promoted transparency, enabled decision-making led by facts and not just intuition or acumen, and changed how we interact both professionally and socially.

Data talks

These days, as they say, data talks and the world listens. We know that data is the new frontier and that it has already asserted itself in corporate life in a major way. Paying attention has never been more important, given the amount of information that is out there.

Take for example a recent global phenomenon: the COVID-19 crisis. It has truly been a time when local response has been critical. Compared to about a hundred years ago, when the world was hit by a similar pandemic—the Spanish flu—during the COVID-19 pandemic we have had the technology to help us in many ways. Analysts have been able to predict trends for the disease, for instance, which has been possible due to large-scale availability of information and data. Technology has also helped many of us to stay connected and continue to work despite being confined to our homes for months.

What lies ahead after the pandemic is over is a question fraught with unknowns, but there are some answers that can be had, thanks to data.

One of the things that is certain is that analytics is changing the way decisions are made. 'Experience and intuition still command a premium but it has been somewhat challenged by analytics and predictive research, which are helping management make informed decisions,' says Manish Bhatia, Managing Director (MD) and Chief Executive Officer (CEO), DIC India Ltd.

Vineet Kumar Kapila, Global Head, Main Stream Spirits, Diageo, agrees. 'I remember twenty years back when we used to run direct routes in Vizag for Coca-Cola India, we found that there were distinct brand preferences across routes. The demand for our brands was not homogeneous in the city. Only if we had the data analytics capability—we could have mined great harvests!'

Nikhil Dey, Executive Director, Adfactors PR, says technology is forcing rapid change in the way organizations are structured and staffed. 'We can already see the impact on society through social media. Cutting through the clutter and finding ways to disrupt the equilibrium have become critical to get attention. It's at the intersection of big, bold, creative ideas and new technology that the answers can be found to bring this to the table.'

Data is the fuel of the economy today. In an article, Bernard Marr writes that 2.5 quintillion bytes of data is produced every single day.[1] And to give you an idea of how fast this number is changing, 'over the last two years alone, 90 per cent of the data in the world was generated', the article clarifies. Everything we do online leaves a digital trail—whether it is sending messages or uploading Instagram stories or making an online purchase. Additionally, all our devices that are busy talking to each other— otherwise known as the internet of things—create their own footprints. And in those footprints lie the details of everyday life—what we want to buy, where we want to go, who we want to be—which companies want to use to reach us more effectively. Is this a good thing for humanity? That is a different question altogether, one that is being debated by activists, ethicists and philosophers. But practically speaking, like it or not, we are all

---

1 'How Much Data Do We Create Every Day? The Mind-Blowing Stats Everyone Should Read', 21 May 2018, *Forbes*, https://www. forbes.com/sites/bernardmarr/2018/05/21/how-much-data-do-we-create-every-day-the-mind-blowing-stats-everyone-should-read/#26f8b66b60ba

part of this giant connected entity that is being watched, the information from which is constantly being put to use.

'Data and understanding its context through artificial intelligence (AI) algorithms will provide corporates with the competitive edge that will be required in the post-COVID-19 world,' says Haresh Hemrajani, MD, Head of Banking, Card and Enterprise Payments Solutions Presales, UK/Europe at FIS. 'The continuous growth and adoption of AI will drive future innovation in products and capabilities. Formulating rules and ethics around data/AI will be equally important as we evolve the algorithms from Artificial Narrow Intelligence (ANI) to Artificial General Intelligence (AGI) and finally to Artificial Superintelligence (ASI).'

'All corporations will be more data driven. Those who will successfully extract information out of data and then make it actionable intelligence will definitely have a competitive edge,' says Sarmila Basu, Senior Director, Data and Decision Sciences, Microsoft. 'In our tech sector, three emerging trends are big data, cloud computing and internet of things. These three together will enable us to solve business problems that we could not even imagine we could solve in the past. From predictive maintenance of machinery, or paediatric cardiac events to AI-based image analysis—the possibilities are endless.'

Anil Nashier, Chief Technology Officer (CTO), COFRA Holding A.G., says, 'We are witnessing the revolutionary phase of technology disruption with capabilities like AI, extended reality and genetic engineering. Technology is going to significantly alter the way consumers, markets and organizations will operate. On the other hand, this could also potentially pose enormous risks for society and human life. It will be pivotal for policymakers to channel technological advancement towards moral empowerment, rather than manipulation. At the same time, the "if it ain't broke, don't fix it" strategy could be lethal, and lack of foresight into the applicability of these capabilities can throw organizations out of business in no time.'

Of course, data has not finished transforming the way we work as yet—it has just gotten started. For now, much of the change that technology is bringing doesn't have the appearance of being at the cutting edge. If you don't look closely, it may seem decidedly mundane. But you'd be wrong.

'From the traditional stand-alone customized software and the occasional enterprise resource planning software which catered to internal process management and financial accounting, businesses now run scores of applications that are all interlinked and connected, inside and outside the organization. Data volumes have increased substantially as the smartphone has helped the masses to connect. Organizations and governments are supporting and driving the digital revolution,' says Manish Gupta, Senior Vice President and Chief Financial Officer (CFO), Member of Board, Mitsubishi Mahindra Agricultural Machinery Co. Ltd.

'We need to be comfortable swimming in a deluge of data,' says Soumen Mukherjee, Partner, Deloitte Netherlands. 'The interconnected world of smart sensors and social media will mean that large volumes of information from disparate sources will suddenly be made available for us to synthesize and make sense of.'

As the data industry grows, it will also evolve, adds Manish Bhatia. 'I believe there will be two capabilities that will command a premium: those who can leverage science to provide more and more accurate analytics and predictive analysis; and those who can interpret unimaginable data to map out a decisive charter for work. The current premium we place on managing data or generating data will just go away as data will be omni-available.'

COVID-19 should not materially impact or derail this continued technological trend, says Haresh Hemrajani. 'As we substitute in-person interactions in a post-COVID-19 world, corporations should leverage data/AI technologies to further enrich their internal portals, knowledge base, business applications and develop lean digital straight-through processes. As corporates adopt more permanent forms of remote working arrangements, the need for AI-based security tooling will play an important role to protect internal data, intellectual property and valued resources.'

If data altered the business landscape in 2020, in the coming decade, its impact is expected to grow ever larger. There will be huge volumes of data and managing it will lead to a set of challenges, which we need to be mindful of. This may further evolve in the future, particularly if the heralded leap in quantum computing arrives and brings an entirely new dimension to how computers work to solve problems. But in either case, AI will fundamentally shift how we look at human productivity. We have now accepted that the future is technology, and technology is the future.

Having done so, what is next for us as we move into this future?

The opportunity

Technology gives; technology takes away. With the rise of automation in all its forms, jobs that are repetitive are believed to be on the verge of extinction. As I mentioned earlier, there are many articles and books on this subject, and as this book is not about how technology will impact our jobs, I will only touch upon what is relevant to our subject.

So, jobs are changing. What's new, you might ask. The past hundred years have seen a complete transformation in how humans produce goods and services. Change is the only constant, after all, so can we predict the future perfectly? Obviously not, but we *can* take a look at what the future holds for us based on what we see today, without pulling out the crystal ball to guess what innovations may be awaiting us.

'Life was never easy and shall never be. The "next thing" is always round the corner. It is like the proverbial ongoing fight between medicos and killer diseases, be it plague, malaria, TB, heart disease, cancer, AIDS and so on. Humans tame one and the next one, even bigger in proportion, pops up … the fight shall always continue.

'Similar is the story of technology and social evolution since time immemorial. Speed at the rate of knots and beyond is the desired pace to cope with the ever-changing environment, systems and culture. Till the "next thing" were to happen, we have got to manage our ways of working or we shall be doomed, and buried in history for our next generation/s to study,' says Puneet Gupta, Managing Director, Franke Faber India Ltd.

Dr P.V. Ramana Murthy, Executive Vice President and Global Head, Human Resources, Taj Hotels, says, 'While there has most certainly been a change in the ways of working in the last decade, I honestly think that the most dramatic change is visible when I compare the workplace of 35 years ago with the workplace today. The pace and quantum of change is dizzying and it is our generation that has had to hold on for the ride! We went from hand-written notes and making presentations using transparencies and projectors to email and WebEx! While I could go on, I will try and address the actual question at hand. Over the last ten years, I have observed that the quest for simplification has gained a steady following. One thing is certain, and that is that life has become more and more complex. People don't have time. It's all about the "it needs to be done yesterday!". Essentially, we need to keep reflecting—on ourselves, our actions and our environments.

While automation had started changing things about a decade ago, the speed at which it has infiltrated every aspect of our lives is astounding. There is no doubt that technology is needed and even essential to simplify life. But we must be mindful that it doesn't take over the thinking, feeling side of humans! While I feel immensely productive when I can obtain accurate information at the click of a button, it is moving to another level where people have stopped thinking for themselves.'

Einstein supposedly quipped that he feared the day technology will surpass our human interaction. Should that happen, he said, the world will have a generation of idiots. Let's hope it doesn't come to that!

Humanity has always moved towards greater efficiency. And it has also frequently resisted the changes that this brings. 'This is of course the big fear about automation—that entry-level repetitive jobs will be scarcer and scarcer in times to come,' says Prabal Mitra, MD, Accenture, Netherlands. 'Automation at the basic level means fewer opportunities for people without special skills.'

Kiran Koteshwar, Chief Financial Officer, SpiceJet Limited says: 'First, the fast-changing work style, work space, decision support systems (DSS) need to be addressed in the context of rapid development in connectivity, computing speeds and process automation. Over the years, we have seen DSS evolve from OHP, to presentations, to Spreadsheet, to Desktop Dashboards to live information and mobile dashboards, on storing information, from files to now Cloud. Similarly on communication and approval processes: from Note Sheets, to Lotus to now work-flow and Online Chat platforms; on matters of product development, from computing market data and information to Big Data analytics and Artificial Intelligence—which have narrowed down consumer preferences and have started predicating future products. These have led to new ways of working, new ways of managing processes, managing governance, selling, and much more. We all need to evolve to keep up with the speed of change.'

Does this mean that we will be talking with humanoid robots across the conference table? No, I hope not. But our machines are becoming smarter and smarter, taking over functions that humans have believed are beyond the scope of a machine. Now we find that not only can technology handle such tasks, but it is even improving performance, and at the very least, freeing up time spent on repetitive tasks for higher-level functions.

On the other hand, it is also true that technology is creating opportunities that were unimaginable when we were in school, preparing plans for our future, completing our education, or rising through the ranks of our first job.

'The pace of change upon us now may be less like evolution and more like a meteor strike, but rather than fear the inevitable, we should learn to coexist with technology,' says Soumen Mukherjee. 'Automation is likely to take away many jobs—but it is also expected to create new roles that do not exist today. The management of a bot farm or imparting emotional intelligence to a software programme will demand newer skills and has triggered a new wave of job creation. It pays not to bemoan the job losses but to appreciate the unique opportunities coming up, and to start training one's mind to make the most of the new skills. The new world of coexistence will separate the winners from the losers not in terms of profits, but in terms of resilience and innovation quotient.'

Change must come, agrees Shridhar Narayan, Group Director and CEO—Infrastructure (Industrial and Logistics), Hiranandani Group. 'The world will continue to become integrated and technological advancement will be the guiding force. The leadership perspective has to undergo a change, given the new world and new demography and the digital revolution. While some look at emerging technologies with fear and anxiety, the most future-ready leaders are excited to integrate them into their workforce.'

There are threats, and there are opportunities. The biggest risk is not that you will not be able to find work, it is that you won't be able to adapt to the work that will be available unless you gear yourself up for the future.

Puneet Gupta sees the world of marketing changing quite fast. 'Old and conventional doctrines, notions and wisdom got challenged. Mobility, internet and "smart everything" has not only changed the way corporates look at product proposition, but the entire working—systems and strategy—has taken a U-turn. For example, the concept of product idea validation, R&D and test-marketing a product in a single geography has been junked completely. From research done with a couple of hundred prospective consumers now, it's about thousands/ millions of "true" interested consumers. Advertising is much beyond "celebrity brand ambassadors" now. It is about a drive, an engagement and a rally with consumers that differentiates one brand from another. Data availability will further reduce helping to better understand consumers and their habits. The so-called competitive advantages for leaders may cease to exist as data will help the catch up much quicker. Perhaps that is the reason start-ups are getting that much attention and resources, unlike before. Good ideas with flawless execution would create many stories even more quickly. New Apple, Microsoft, Google, Facebook could erupt from nowhere and in no time.'

'People often are worried about technology, thinking it will replace humans. My take is that it will only reduce certain types of jobs as we will also need a lot more humans who can programme the machine,' says Sarmila Basu of Microsoft.

Of course, machines have been replacing humans in the workplace for some time now. Automation has been around, and it has been efficient even when it wasn't what we would call intelligent.

I have always found technology to be fascinating as it isn't always what we expect it to be. Having been brought up on a diet of science fiction where robots look and sound like slightly stilted and awkward humans, I wonder how will the future look like with such speedy advent of technology.

'We live in fascinating times—a period that is likely to be described as the third industrial revolution,' says Jayesh Desai, former Head of Investment, Piramal Enterprises Ltd.

Now we have reached a juncture where technology may take over jobs that humans have always considered sacrosanct—jobs that depend on human judgement, intellect and artistry. As far back as 1968, Lewis R. Goldberg demonstrated how a simple algorithm could outperform doctors in diagnosing correctly and consistently cases of malignant versus benign cancers.[2] And now, fifty years later, technologies like this are finally being deployed in the real world. AI is being used as a diagnostic aid in many other medical fields.

New technologies will affect the entire life cycle of a product, from development through production. 'Usage of technology and in particular AI will change the process and speed of identifying changing consumer needs, optimized supply chain models will make it faster and easier to manufacture and distribute the products, and better analytics will help track consumer reactions and complaints,' says Sandeep Batra, CFO, Crompton Greaves Consumer Electricals.

Ashok Cherian, Chief Information Officer (CIO), Page Industries, is hoping to see a day when he will be 'supervised by a robo-boss'!

---

2   'Simple Models or Simple Processes? Some Research on Clinical Judgments', *American Psychologist*, 23, no. 7.

'We all are used to seeing robots in an automotive production line, but now they are coming into many other job profiles outside of it,' he says.

'Cognitive computing platforms like IBM Watson are evolving,' points out Manish Gupta, 'taking over and surpassing human capabilities for tasks which still are dominated and considered suitable for humans only.' Kiran Koteshwar says, 'The current professionals who in the last ten years must have seen a revolution in communication, data and information processing, and analytics have adapted to the ever-changing environment. Those who haven't must have been relegated to oblivion, and if not, then the business they run must have been doomed. We have been adapting and developing skill sets. But I have seen that it's not enough; we are seriously lacking a focussed approach toward getting retrained to fully utilize these technological advancements; and for those who have, then they face resistance by "fixed mindsets".'

Those of us in old-world industries read about developments such as AI as a thing of the future and it all seems rather far away. But it shouldn't. The very fact that the top four out of five companies in terms of global market cap are technology companies (Microsoft, Apple, Amazon and Alphabet) shows how the world has changed in the past decades. The older biggies have moved down the list and are struggling to survive the avalanche unleashed by the technology-oriented, agile and forward-looking players. And it's not just happening at the top—the fight is out in the open at all levels; it is the very DNA of companies that is changing, in every nook and corner of the globe.

And all this occurred even before COVID-19 hit. 'The pandemic has brought economic disruption of enormous proportions and has been more severe and occurred much faster than anything else in recorded economic history,' says Dilip Pal, CFO, Safaricom PLC. Our beliefs and assumptions of the world have changed dramatically since then. But we have also witnessed an unprecedented wave of innovation and creativity driven by new methods and tools. In a conversation with Lulu Garcia- Navarro, historian Yuval Noah Harari said, "That conviction that people held for years and decades and seemed to be completely set in stone can actually be overturned very quickly in such a situation."[3] The whole existential crisis also favoured deep introspection and led many companies to transform themselves not only to survive but thrive in the new era. Automation and robots are changing the way businesses operate with amazing speed and on a scale beyond belief just a few years ago. The corporate world has adapted to the change with a strong belief that things will never return to normal.'

Demands of digital transformation

With this shift and the opportunities created by technology, the question then is: Can any organization stay away from digital transformation?

The answer is a resounding 'no'. It is more critical than ever to take the leap. If your company has not taken its digital transformation journey yet, this may be the last and final boarding call.

'Billions of people are connected today, and we have unprecedented processing power and knowledge access. Far too much data is available and is being analysed for reading consumer trends in the search for incremental revenue and

---

3   https://www.npr.org/2020/04/05/827582502/a-historian-looks-ahead-at-a-transformed-post-pandemic-world

managing costs,' says Sunil Gupta, CFO, Bottling Investments Group, The Coca-Cola Company. This makes adapting to new technologies a matter of survival. 'Business disruptions are faster than ever. Correspondingly, chances of survival are dimmer unless firms are ahead of the curve in the space of AI, big data and advanced analytics,' he says. 'There is so much that can be achieved through the use of data for incremental revenue opportunities, enhanced efficiencies and lower costs. Digital capital is fast becoming equally if not more important for businesses, alongside economic and human capital. Companies which build a significant competitive advantage by (a) training and retraining their people; and (b) by institutionalizing the internal processes and decision-making based on usage of data, will see their investment in digital and data analytics pay them multifold and provide an inherent competitive advantage.'

Technology is progressing at an unprecedented pace, and we can see the change occurring before our very eyes. As we have seen, some companies have already started making full use of technology and are ensuring that their workforces are equipped to deal with the change.

At this stage, there is no place for tokenism. 'Digital transformation must be brought about as a strategic business change and business driver, rather than piecemeal change in the form of websites, social media and other platforms,' says Manish Gupta. We will see this in action more and more as a new generation of companies rises to the top in this era. 'Consumers are becoming digitally savvy and that is reflected by their lifestyles. The organizations that harness this aspect of consumer lifestyles will be successful in leading others. In the current fast-paced business environment and lean organizational structure, leaders need to learn and embrace new technologies. The current change is a paradigm shift, just like we experienced with the evolution of computers in the early 1980s. Leaders of our times will go through the same phenomenon and the more tech savvy ones will move into the future and be successful,' he says.

'Most business models will be disrupted, and this will mean that professional services firms will need to rethink their offerings,' says Sanjesh Thakur, Partner, Deloitte India. 'AI, machine learning and analytics which, until a year back, sounded like specialized skills, will be common to perform routine operations.'

Sunil Gupta says, 'Many times I see leaders jump into the bandwagon of digital/advanced analytics without really fully understanding and defining the picture of success. They end up spending millions of dollars behind projects led by technology consultants with little or no payback.

'Digital transformation is a must, but the key is to define the end goals and build a group of business leaders within the organization who will be the flag bearers of these initiatives. Like most things in life, usage breeds familiarity and familiarity breeds comfort. The larger organization falls in line once the benefits are visible.

'The corporations with first-mover advantage are likely to be significant gainers over those who will just be followers.'

Ashish Aul, Partner, KPMG India, points out that there has been a massive surge in expectation towards the use of technology post COVID-19, thanks to working from home. And this will only continue. 'The way disruptions are happening, digital transformation is the way to go across businesses, and hence, it is important to have a long-term technology strategy for future disruptions and changes in the business environment. Already we have seen organizations enhancing their digital footprint and accelerating efforts in this direction.'

Sandeep Batra says, 'The pace of change in the overall economic framework, e.g., Brexit, changes in regulatory framework, changes due to technological advances, such as Robotics, AI and Blockchain, will push the corporate world towards further transformations and be more mindful and cautious in order to ensure stakeholders are not dealt with "casually". The way the regulations around sustainability of operations are being strengthened, organizations which will fail to adopt the new wave or are late to adopt could well become extinct. In our industry, we have a revolution with the advent of LED technology in lighting products. Thanks to the Government's intervention and drive, LED bulbs have seen very healthy adoption rates. The usage has grown exponentially. Companies which resisted this change have seen their business shrink, and those which embraced this change are flourishing. Such trends of digital adaptation will continue. Business models will have to be lean and flexible to adapt to such changes.'

The journey towards automating tasks had already begun in the pre-COVID era, as per Dilip Pal. However, the current crisis has accelerated some of these changes. 'Digital transformation has become a must and, in some companies, a question of survival. There are many examples of this: chatbots are being rapidly introduced for varied degrees of customer interaction. No one could imagine that call centre agents could work-from-home (WFH) to serve customers; this was possible through technological advancement. More and more consumers are interacting through digital platforms rather than face-to-face. Robots and intelligent machines will replace physical labour in many fields. Radical acceleration is happening across the globe to embed technology.'

As per Anil Nashier, 'Digital transformation, for organizations, is a journey that could either target transforming/disrupting an entire business model or staying competitive by means of offering innovative digital products and services. Digitalization and being a digital business could altogether be a different ball game. It is very important to recognize the true sense of your own digital ambition. A digital transformation is a step change and is fundamentally different from the concept of continuous improvements for marginal improvements over time.'

Digitization and new emerging technologies will create new horizontal bands that will cut across the organization, and perhaps be the most disruptive trend going ahead, agrees Himal Tiwari, Chief Human Resource Officer, Tata Power Ltd. While we will see a lot of process-related enablement through technology and digitization, there will also be the emergence of subject matter experts who will feed in the knowledge software on this new hardware, he says.

'We are increasingly becoming more horizontal from being vertical for our working and efficiency,' says Manish Bhatia. 'A brand marketeer can't work without digital, a digital manager can't work without content from a brand manager, a retail salesperson may have a pay-at-store target for which sales happened online. All of this is leading to networking and collaboration skills becoming as important as being a domain expert ... Expertise today is available through AI platforms; the only thing which these platforms can't do today is seamlessly and in real-time collaborate, which is fundamentally where our new ways of working need to evolve.' While companies will have to respond to this shift at an institutional level, we look at the individual response to these changes in the next section.

Some industries have been moving faster than others in developing disruptive technology, bringing about uneven change. 'The financial services industry has been an early adapter to the changing world,' believes Jayesh Desai. 'For instance, if you look at traditional banking in India, private sector banks are moving at a very fast pace to adopt technology. Banks now boast about being able to sanction loans in less than a minute, all thanks to technology.' Risk assessment, credit score prediction and fraud detection are just some of the uses for advanced technology in the banking sector.

Syed Safawi, former Managing Director and Group Chief Executive Officer, VLCC, puts his view differently and says, 'GREED' is going to define our industries as well as the corporate world. However, this greed can be described as:

G: Geo-politics is beginning to have an impact on the future of business, including the start of trade wars.
R: Data will become almost the religion.
E: Economic shifts to India and China as global economic centres will change the corporate thought process over the next few decades.
E: Evolution towards industries and their business models.
D: Design (as against just technology) will be the next frontier.

The industrial sector is not far behind, and is moving towards full automation across the board, says Pranesh Chatterjee, Manager, Technology, Projects and Strategy, Tata Steel Europe. 'In terms of data speed, mobile usage, data volume and embedded devices, the future of communication is indeed all about technology—to drive growth and business forward. The internet of things will reign supreme over all other means of communication, based on which the industry will flourish.'

Sanjesh Thakur, Partner, Deloitte India says, 'Technology has occupied the centre stage in our lives, creating this hyper-connected world that we live in. It is at the intersection of all business discussions/decisions and the lines between core IT function and business are getting blurred. For example, if we flashback, emails have taken the place of letters and memos and messages; WhatsApp has taken the place of emails.

'With technology, the speed of business communication has significantly increased. The volume of data and information has multiplied and the attention span of business executives has reduced across the board. For example, people expect response to emails on the same day and in most cases the next few hours, barring a few cases with the time zone difference.

'Professionals have moved from being the "hard worker" to becoming an "innovative/smart worker". This is also leading to managers being challenged on leadership practices based on traditional ways of working or history. The other day, I was sitting in a business meeting where a retail store manager proposed to his supervisor that across all the upcoming stores, the changing room should have ambient lighting as most of the buy/no buy decisions in the apparel business are made there. It is great to see that people have increasingly started to question known patterns. In the process, we are increasingly becoming an outcome-driven innovative organization.' We have focused mainly on aspects of changing technology that are already being adopted. This is because, over the years, experts have never been entirely accurate in trying to predict how technology will change our future. We aren't all printing out flying cars on our 3D printers and setting them off into the sunset, are we? Our hopes—and fears—about technology have always, in every era, been partly correct and partly exaggerated and optimistic. So let us keep our eyes and ears open as we continue adapting to the needs of the future. Wouldn't that be more prudent?

2
Reimagining Work

Finding purpose and balance

For the new generation workforce, it is no longer only about work. People are looking for a holistic life. It is not about selling their time for a salary at the cost of missing out on the rest of life. People are mostly united in demanding that the world prioritizes balance of life with work, profit with purpose. Most are in search of deeper meaning in their work. Purpose is not only important for today's organizational mottos, it plays a big role in talent deciding if they would like to be associated with a company. When the purpose of an organization or leadership resonates with their own purpose, it all falls into place.

'The new workforce is clear in its thought process and vocal about its perspectives on life,' says Ashish Aul, Partner, KPMG

India. 'The new generation doesn't want to carry on with the legacy or traditional mindset and has a fresh outlook on life, career and relationships. It is that purpose which keeps us moving and finding motive in our day-to-day lives. For me, the purpose has to be beyond achieving material benefit or recognition; it cannot be something that is transactional. The new generation is moving on the right track, I would say.'

Anurabh Das Sharma, former President, Bennett Coleman and Co. Ltd, says, 'In my view, in the future, I think people will value mere number of years of experience a lot less and skills a lot more. Just because I have grey hair—which, by the way, I have—and have worked for twenty-five years, people will not necessarily take what I say seriously unless they find value in my words. The future is all about skills over experience.'

The discussion on work–life balance has been on the table for some time, says Indraneel Roy Choudhury, Partner, PWC India, but it's been brought into focus by COVID-19. 'People have been expected to be in their virtual offices, colleges or schools at all times. The pressure is now, more than earlier, in these work-from-home days. The need for finding a purpose for life amidst this disruption has grown stronger.'

Sandeep Batra adds, 'While the world may describe these changes as revolutionary, in my humble opinion, these will be evolutionary. When I started working 30 years back, the world was a very different place. But the changes that took place, while appearing at the point in time to be revolutionary, now appear to be a part of an evolution. If I, and many people around me, could adapt to those changes, so would the leaders of tomorrow, and they will adopt. Needless to say, only the fittest will survive, but that remains the rule of the corporate jungle. Hence, we need to constantly upskill and outskill.'

The new-age digital world has changed the face of globalization and blurred borders and even generations, says Sameer Agarwal, CFO, Manipal Health Enterprises Pvt. Ltd. 'The millennials want to use their skills to benefit a cause. They also seem to be moving away from buying physical assets like a house or car, and seem to be leaning towards a more experience-driven lifestyle.'

The shift is a significant one. 'People once said they worked for money, power and position, recognition and creation. That can be a theory of the past,' says Satyakam Basu, External Advisor, Bain and Company. 'The new workforce will be quite different; they believe that the very purpose of life is to find its purpose, and they are ready to accept and adapt to change.' The new workforce would also like to anticipate the change that is coming as early as possible and master it, says Basu. 'They would like to be part of the change waves, if not the change agent itself.' Sanjesh Thakur says, 'At a macro level, companies having an authentic and genuine purpose with stakeholders and employees will have a great source of competitive advantage. I think the workforce of the future will look for more and more 'purpose' in what they are doing. The impact they are creating through their work will matter more than just the pay cheque they earn. In my view, the next-generation workforce will place a far greater emphasis on work culture and flexibility and not just pay. Corporations and business leaders need to be in sync with their priorities which could be around improving ways of working, improving the society in general, and caring for the planet, in addition to just generating profits.'

Call for authenticity

With transparency in policies and processes supported by the huge amount of information available, the new world has manifested a need for authenticity. 'Never before have we sought "truth" over "fake" with so much passion,' says Deepa Dey, Head, Communications and Sustainability, Nutrition and Special Projects, Hindustan Unilever Limited. This is perhaps more critical as organizations become reliant on their communication to reach their consumers: fake does not read well on social platforms. With the rise of the influencers, at least the appearance of a connection with a brand is increasingly important.

The demand for authenticity also comes from organizations listening to consumers through all the channels that have now opened up. 'It is not one-way communication—there is a big feeling of being able to communicate back. It is a conversational approach,' says Ravi Sahgal, Executive Vice President and Business Head, Kurlon Limited.

'Data usage has gone up manifold and is creating transparency. Mass awareness has become so high that no one can hide behind non-authenticity anymore,' says Diptendu Mondal, Director Sourcing, Ericsson.

During COVID-19, with times as challenging as they are, the need for authenticity has only increased. Many brands have steered clear of communication during this time, for fear of striking the wrong note. They do not want to continue as though it is business-as-usual, and so have pulled their planned communication. Though people want to hear from brands, particularly about products and services that are important at this time, the messaging needs to be real, useful and sensitive.

As an appliance manufacturer in India discovered to its detriment, it chose to advertise its roti maker—a useful gadget in an India that suddenly had to cope with doing chores without domestic help—by suggesting that the hands of maids may be infected. The backlash was swift and unanimous, and the company withdrew the ad. While such advertising is never acceptable, bearing in mind that the ongoing crisis affects every strata of society, it was particularly egregious.

And it isn't just authenticity in marketing: it is a value that has become important to organizations themselves, and hence to leadership. 'We are increasingly seeing leaders being more connected across the organization, becoming more real and approachable. Values like authenticity and vulnerability are becoming new virtues for leaders,' says Himal Tiwari. This has arisen as both a cause and an effect of changing corporate structures.

If the company pursues authenticity, so must its leaders. 'The topmost quality I admire in any leader is the bet they place on people—a leader who stands by his people, encourages and motivates them and creates a safety net to fall in. A leader has to walk the talk and set an example by demonstrating such values to navigate through these complex and challenging times. He or she needs to be authentic and transparent,' says Ashish Aul.

Indraneel Roy Choudhury agrees. 'This is absolutely right, more so in view of the lack of trust in establishments, institutions and leadership across the world. The trust deficit has come to the fore with the pandemic and the best way to address it is always with clear, transparent communication. One may not like what is being said or the way things are handled, but the stamp of transparency creates trust.'

Let us also look at how the workplace is adopting such changes.

Taking guard

It was in the midst of this already-changing world that the novel coronavirus erupted across the globe through the course of 2020, forcing us to adapt overnight to a new normal. I believe that, as a phenomenon, COVID-19 will pass, but it will change the world and the way we operate, live and lead for good.

No one can deny that while COVID-19 has thrown many challenges before us, it has also opened up new perspectives and opportunities, and has taught us to look at life and work differently. Some of these changes are here to stay, while others may disappear in the coming months and years, as countries enter different stages in their fight against the pandemic. We don't know yet how that will pan out.

One of my biggest learnings from COVID-19 is how technology has helped us continue with life as usual in some functions or sectors. While the inability to physically be in the workplace has affected many sectors, such as airlines, travel and tourism, and manufacturing, many other industries and functions have demonstrated their ability to operate smoothly even during the crisis. And this has been possible only due to the leap we have taken globally through technology.

'Every crisis opens up an opportunity to rethink the way we imagined our world,' says Prriti Narain, HR Lead, GBO Sales, Google, USA. 'Adaptability, innovation and agility are the skills of the new world that are imperative to survive. The world is adapting in two ways, and one is more at the surface. Yes, work-from-home does work for most corporates, especially in the short run. It works more on the back of existing relationships that the larger organization has already established. It works on the back of a culture or values that an organization embodies. It also works more effectively in some sectors than in others due to the nature of work. These are a fortunate few.'

But, adds Prriti, at a broader economic level, there is a definite need for greater preparedness. 'Traditional businesses were caught off-guard and were not ready to deal with a crisis of this magnitude. There is certainly an opportunity to revisit some of our age-old practices, such as a dependence on a workforce that survives on daily or contract work, with no institutional support. The unorganized sector forms the backbone of our economic structure. There is a need for a framework that ensures the security and sustenance of the worker, and safeguards the interest of the corporate entity employing this workforce. This will also ensure that economic activity is not disrupted. COVID-19 has taught us these lessons.'

Ramanan G.V., Vice President Finance and Group Controller, Tata Motors Ltd says, 'Most of the important things in our personal and professional life start with "C": cash, compliance, challenge, care, comfort, co-existence, compassion and now COVID-19. But one Big C that underlines all these is Change. Change is the only constant in life.

'Reactions to change vary from company to company and individual to individual. The one who accepts it, does things differently, is more adaptable to change and succeeds in the new environment.

'Change is a constant and is something we experience right from our childhood: change of schools, change of teachers, change of cities that we live in, change of houses, change of friends. In all these experiences, we have done well. Then why does change become a herculean task as we grow up?'

'As we grow and climb up the professional ladder of success, comfort slowly sets in, as well as an element of fear. We begin to resist change. It starts with an unwillingness to accept change, learn new things, walk the unknown path. We then always need an incentive to change—"what is in it for me?"—career growth, better remuneration, higher band/designation. These incentives then drive our reaction to change.

'It is important to view change from the lens of learning and knowledge. This will make individuals and companies a lot more resilient to change and help embrace change successfully.'

The long-term consequences of COVID-19 to industries and society will extend far beyond crisis management, and unless companies realize this, there will be aftershocks. 'COVID-19 poses a two-stage challenge to the corporate world: it starts with crisis management, and charts its way towards opportunity management as the duration of this crisis is prolonged,' says Haresh Hemrajani. 'Unfortunately, not all corporates have recognized this second challenge. A lot has been addressed and publicized to promote team communication, collaboration, remote team management and aligning facilities to promote health and safety of employees. However, COVID-19 also requires corporates to reimagine their respective businesses in the post-COVID-19 era. It is an unavoidable consequence that some business models will be disrupted permanently in the post-COVID-19 era.'

Moving office

Office is no longer a specific space where you go every morning to work. Remote working is here to stay.

In my long career, I never worked from home continuously for three months, and never even imagined it would be possible with my global responsibilities. Many around me felt the same. The forced lockdown due to COVID-19 showed us that it is indeed possible, and studies have shown that in most cases, productivity has not dropped.

Even before COVID-19 hit the world, work-from-home was on the rise, agrees Rajesh Dangi, CTO, NxtGen Infinite Datacenter, and with it the use of collaboration tools such as Slack, Meets and Zoom. This means downtime is a thing of the past. Conference calls, all day every day, even when driving, is the new normal.

Sreenivasa Rao Yadavilli, former Managing Director India, Korn Ferry Futurestep, says, 'COVID-19 will dramatically change work cultures, management styles and the concept of work environment. What would have taken twenty years or so has been fast-tracked by nature. I am willing to argue that most corporates have not yet woken up to the structural changes COVID-19 will leave behind. Once the business existence cash issues are sorted, corporates will find themselves in a new alien land. My belief is that upto 75 per cent of the workforce in knowledge industries and "not working with hands" industries will move to work from "anywhere". I'm not sure if it will be work-from-home per se. I believe humans are social beings and one of the drivers of a career/job is the social bonding, competitiveness, human emotive expressions, and most importantly, the learning from work social interactions, which might lead to a huge rise in "near home" third-party/ independent rented office spaces. My guess is 20–30 per cent of the "anywhere" work employees will choose to work from "near office" facilities. I see a future where a vast majority will work from places they can walk to from home.

'Both the work-from-home and "near office" environments will throw up totally new challenges and management concerns. The most important factor will be employee engagement and a sense of belonging to an organization. Second is going to be supervision and "monitoring" performance. Third is going to be real-time course correction. Fourth is peer group learning. Fifth and most important is going to be culture.'

As Prriti Narain points out, many organizations were already headed in this direction. 'COVID-19 has only accelerated this process, forcing many companies to adapt digitally and culturally to this new world. WFH and flexitime will definitely be more commonly acceptable than in the past and hence, will open up more avenues of employment for many people who were earlier unable to participate in the workforce due to constraints, for example, people with disabilities, or those who are caregivers at home.'

With the idea of the workplace being expanded so dramatically, national borders can no longer hold people back. 'Technology is allowing us to work a lot more collaboratively, making it possible for us to work with our colleagues remotely,' says Sarmila Basu. 'We are always connected. The traditional concept of working long hours sitting in the office is long gone, everyone is always on.'

Gopi Koteeswaran, CEO, LatentView, says that this would not have been possible a decade ago. 'I appreciate the fact that now I can be contacted and can respond to any work emergency even if I am not at my office. However, this improved connectivity also proves a challenge to truly disconnect from work and enjoy personal time.'

'Over time I can see a shrinking office space and even time-shared office space. The shift has already started,' says Kiran Koteshwar. Naveen Begwani, Vice President and Controller-EMEA, Kohler Co., points out that while the world has seen many crises in the past hundred years, it has also witnessed many positive disruptions in the field of communication and technology, which have changed the ways of working for all businesses. 'During this time of crisis, resilience and response has been equally befitting. Within a period of weeks, the entire world equipped itself with the tools and technology to enable seamless work-from-home. The question has not been just about resuming work, but also working effectively and efficiently by maintaining the same level of productivity.'

Surajit Banerjee, Senior Vice President and Head-HR, SpiceJet Ltd, says that COVID-19 has prompted organizations to differentiate between operational roles requiring physical presence and others that can be done in the work-from-home mode. 'WFH is a necessity now and is likely to emerge as an important option in most organizations in the future,' he says. 'Employees are also developing significant comfort with it.'

Dr P.V. Ramana Murthy says, 'Offices could become a thing of the past—work–life balance will be replaced with work–health balance. Pensions will become a thing of the past because today, one can work for 40 years at the most. Going forward, this will change to 50 or even 60 years due to a change in life expectancy, advances in medicine and changes in social policies, among other factors. The new generation, which has had different and varied experiences while growing up, will care more about sustainability and, flexibility and will believe in getting the job done on their own time, in their own style, with a purpose-driven life.' The workplace restructure is here to stay, says Dilip Pal, and he sees several benefits. 'Firstly, there is a need to restructure the workplace in a way that minimizes close human contact. Our fear of being infected with a virus will never go away. Secondly, there is consensus that employees have been far more productive working from home. Finally, working from home has huge financial benefits for corporates, which they will find hard to ignore.' We may not continue exactly as we are now, but 'flexible ways of work will prevail', he adds. This will be enabled by ever-more sophisticated and advanced automation tools.

The tools will enable our move into a hybrid future, agrees Ramanan G.V., Vice President Finance and Group Controller, Tata Motors Ltd. 'Digital tools are being adopted during this time by companies as most are trying to help their employees adjust to WFH. In the future, there will be an increase in WFH/flexitime as a hybrid working environment will be best for everyone.'

Amidst all the challenges presented by the coronavirus, Diptendu Mondal points out that organizations have seen benefits too, thanks to reduced travel costs, hotel expenditures and reduced fixed operating expenditures. 'Probably no company would have been comfortable about taking on this type of a cost-reduction project under normal circumstances. Many resources who are successfully operating for months from home will continue to do so, as many companies have already decided. On the other hand, people will be able to spend more time with family and this will help work–life balance. It would be a win-win situation going forward for both employee and employer.'

At the technology firm BRIDGEi2i Analytics Solutions, the entire business with 600 employees went remote over one weekend, explains Monideepa Bhattacharya, the firm's Director of Business Development. 'This was phenomenal, given the level of technology complexity, data privacy and client virtual spaces we needed to deal with. Coupled with testing, access issues from multiple cities, client readiness and tech upgrades, this was a mammoth job that happened without one glitch. I think it took everyone by surprise!'

Extraordinary times call for extraordinary measures, adds Bhattacharya. 'It's been an interesting time to see reactions of the corporate world to a black swan event such as COVID-19. In many ways, everyone is living a historic moment. Since the Second World War, be it the financial crisis of 2008 or the recessionary winds in many countries, no event has put the corporate world under greater pressure and in greater uncertainty than this pandemic. On the work-from-home front, we have the pandemic to thank for this push into a model that has been in existence for a long time, but hasn't been able to override the perceived benefit and requirement of being "on the floor" at all times.'

Being pushed into work-from-home en masse is not easy for companies or employees, as it robs people of choice, she says. 'However, drastic changes to operating models possibly happen best, drastically.'

The very idea of what constitutes work has changed. 'The new world demands a willingness to disassociate the traditional concept of "work" from "payroll"—as the digital ecosystem creates a new breed of "workers" who are neither blue collared, nor white collared! And they are adept at working from anywhere for anyone,' says Soumen Mukherjee.

At no other time in history other than during the COVID-19 pandemic has the ability to work remotely been so important. Companies across the world have allowed employees to work exclusively from home, even mandated it in many cases. And it is not only particular industries where working from home is already the norm; it is all industries, even those that had stubbornly clung to the notion that their work required all staff to be in office at all times to function properly. Advertising agencies, media houses and banks have all embraced the WFH culture and suddenly realized that it is indeed possible to work from different locations collaboratively with as much efficiency.

And they seem to be embracing this change for the longer term. IBM, which employs over 1,00,000 people across India, has decided to give up half of its 10 million square foot office space across the country.[4] HDFC and IndusInd Bank have downsized too.[5] TCS has announced that only 25 per cent of the workforce will work from premises by 2025.

Workplaces may never be the same again. Do we also see a change in the way our workforce will view their ways of working?

---

4   https://tech.economictimes.indiatimes.com/news/corporate/ibm-plans-to-reduce-office-space-by-nearly-half-in-india/76447663

5   https://www.livemint.com/companies/news/it-firms-banks-let-go-of-prime-real-estate-in-bid-to-cut-fixed-costs-11589484854711.html

Flexibility is the new norm

Many leaders do predict that our ways of working will change. This change will not only be in the location of work but will also be about being flexible and adaptable; it will be in the way we interact, the way we lead and deal with people.

The focus will be on output.

Technology has already challenged our traditional notions of career. It has connected us, making the world accessible to most of us. It has created opportunities to do business beyond our physically accessible territory. It has helped us work from anywhere, not just confined to a physical space called office, and yet has allowed us to realize our corporate dreams.

I remember my parents always wanted me to have a government job, to be part of the administrative service. The thought arose from a sense of insecurity, since they believed government jobs to be more secure than private ones as the hire-and-fire tradition does not apply to the former. But when I started my career in the private sector, the advice was, stick to your job, a rolling stone gathers no moss.

I appreciated their concerns and thought process given the economic conditions and thinking of the time, but I went on to work in five industries, each of which helped me gain immense exposure. I'm not sure how much moss I gathered, but I certainly do not regret my moves.

Today, as I look at the next generation, I find my thoughts are obsolete thanks to the popularity of the gig economy. Many youngsters today believe in their freedom and are clear about how they want to live, how they would like to divide their time between work and other things in life. This phenomenon that has erupted over the past decade is a trend we should expect to stay and grow. We now have workers who can work from anywhere; and anywhere might means a coffee shop in Bangalore or a beach shack in the Caribbean. Digital nomads are on the rise.

Ravi Sahgal says, 'It is hence very important to remain relevant. Leaders will have to, in many ways, be more acceptable and current with the thinking of the 'doers' and 'followers'— not the other way around, as opposed to what we have seen through grown-up corporate leaders. In simple terms, the ways of work have changed, and technology has been one of the most important factors to enable such change. Studies say that after COVID-19, when the economy settles down again, there will be a rise in deep flexible expertise as organizations will move away from fixed labour cost to flexible labour cost.

'Trust and performance-based culture will define post-COVID-19 leadership,' says Dilip Pal. 'Flexible ways of working will require frequent communication, engagement and collaboration with clear guidelines on goals, expectation and systematic follow-up. Managers need to focus more on objectives/goals and let employees manage their time.'

Prabal Mitra, Managing Director, Accenture, Netherlands, predicts a change in the mix of the workforce, a shift from permanent employment to more need- and skill-based employment. 'As companies become more platform-centric, there will be a movement away from permanent contracts to temporary, skill-based engagements,' he says.

The last few years, feels Soumen Mukherjee, have already redefined the way work and careers are shaped—and this will only continue. 'The digital world is likely to see "cartographic careers"—where the map of career will move across longitudes of diverse skills. But some of the foundational skills that academics and upbringing impart to everyone will forever be relevant.'

Not only will organizations with vision explore flexible work timings, says Sarojit Banerjee, they will also seek flexibility in the mode of people deployment, utilization and terms of employment.

Work-from-home has allowed the concept of flexitime to be more institutionalized. Employees may choose to work from home some days, some of the time. Or they may choose to work hours that fall outside the conventional 9 a.m. to 6 p.m. In fact, with people being able to work from anywhere anytime, I know some who are thinking of moving away from cities to live closer to nature. All they need is a private space with a good internet and telephone connection to remain efficient and deliver. And, obviously, some good coffee.

If this means freedom for everyone to decide, it also means employees need to be disciplined and task-focused as they manage their own time, with no one directly overseeing what they are up to during work hours. This means a change in mindset for each of us and the ability to adapt to such change. 'With disaggregated teams and work-from-home cultures, it is important to have team members who are self-driven and disciplined. Bosses are no longer watching over the shoulder to see progress on projects,' says Vineet Kapila of Diageo.

Does this mean more free time or time with the family? Will this help some women stay in the workforce when motherhood might have otherwise pulled them away? Will this allow fathers to share the responsibility of parenting? Or does this mean longer hours and a never-ending work schedule? Only time will tell.

Creeping in of virtual fatigue

I started thinking about virtual fatigue as COVID-19 set in during early 2020. I wrote an article in which I asked readers three questions … (1) Do you recognize the possibility of virtual fatigue? (2) If yes, should we leave this issue to be tackled by individuals or should we step in as leaders? (3) If we should, what steps will you take to help your team avoid virtual fatigue?

In my view, the new world with its new rules will challenge our mental and physical health in novel ways. I call this virtual fatigue. And if we do not learn to take care of ourselves and the people around us individually and collectively, we will be heading towards serious trouble.

I am not a physician, but as I understand from my doctor friends, virtual fatigue is a kind of fatigue or tiredness that has long-term effects on the human body and mind. It occurs from continuously performing tasks and interacting virtually and can lead to a loss of energy, productivity and agility.

We humans are social beings and are used to freedom of movement. We are not used to remaining confined to one place for weeks or months on end. Living and working in the same place with no other outlets is not the usual way of living for us and might lead to complications for some of us, be they physical or mental.

Virtual fatigue is causing stress or even burnout in people. This could then lead to significant social impact in the form of conflicts, loss of self-confidence, loss of self-esteem, drop in productivity, lack of job satisfaction and other impacts that could have long-term effects on our society and organizations. If this new milieu were to continue for a long time, its effects could become more pronounced.

The article attracted a lot of feedback from industry leaders. Their comments shed further light on this issue. Below are some of their responses.

Monideepa Bhattacharya of BRIDGEi2i Analytics Solutions: 'I have been working from home for ten years now, across different types of roles. Battling perception, lack of face-to face interactions, multitasking with home and childcare responsibilities isn't easy. I ended up inventing many ways of being productive, and even making new relationships at work. But I had made a choice. When WFH suddenly stops becoming a matter of choice, I can see how some people would struggle. It is all about balancing your life.'

Steve Rudderham, Head of GBS, AkzoNobel: 'One of the things that works for me is getting into a routine and sticking to that structure. I still wear a suit even when I work from home. It engages my brain and gets me ready for the day ahead. I think that not having this structure adds to this tiredness and also the demotivation factor.'

Suvam Banerjee, Program Clinical Data Manager/Project Manager at DOCS International Germany GmbH: 'Largely, our problems are thought-driven. The idea of being tied up at home is creating a wave of discomfort which shouldn't be the case if someone knows how to keep distance from his thoughts. This is the time to reflect on our inner wellbeing.'

Arvind Mane, Co-founder and Managing Partner, GV Consultants: 'Indeed, virtual fatigue will set in unless we invest in mental health. After all, humans are social animals.'

Devesh Jain, Partner, EY: 'My experience is that I am getting stressed but not tired (because physical activity is so less). This has also led to less sleep and further stress. Every day, I need to lead my day with an end in mind to avoid any procrastination.'

Puneet Gupta, Managing Director, Franke Faber India Ltd: With demand vs supply matrix for talent moving in favour of supply ... we got to learn to manage stress or perish very quickly. "Burnt out" cases will be on the upswing ... this is Darwin's theory of evolution playing out in corporate life like never before. Spiritual strength and physical fitness are the pre-requisites for survival.'

Neeraj Bhalla, Vice President and Head Digital Centre, Mahindra and Mahindra Ltd: 'As leaders we must try different things. My team got together on a virtual weekend from home for a fun evening! With sundowners! Each one in the team also has a target to learn something new, whatever it is, through Coursera or Udemy or whatever. Let's challenge ourselves to reimagine the future.'

Arunabha Ghosh, Head, Oracle Presales, EAS (Europe), TCS: 'Virtual fatigue is connected to decision fatigue, crisis fatigue and many more sources of stress. We are social beings and many of our decisions—good or bad—are conceptualized when we interact socially. Our decisions are triggered not just through the auditory process, but also through our other senses. How is the other person reacting to my actions? Absence of these affect our decision-making ability and drains mental energy as the day goes by, resulting in decision fatigue.

'At the same time, we are unsure of what lies ahead. No matter how optimistic a person is, the uncertainty around health and economy is creating a sense of crisis at the back of our minds and the resulting fatigue is detrimental. Put these together and you have John Maxwell's definition of a crisis: "An intense time of difficulty requiring a decision that will be a turning point." And leaders have huge pressure to make significant, difficult decisions quickly. Now more than ever.

'How do we avoid ending up in that vortex? Don't forget the basic tenets of human civilization: continue to be socially active and continue challenging your mind. Do check your decisions ahead of time with someone whom you trust. Lean on someone who can lend their shoulder if you feel drained out. And realize, your team members are also humans like you and reach out to them exactly in the same way as you would like to be reached out to.'

What does any of this mean for the workforce of the future? Many experts tell us that adopting new skills is a must. However, years of experience, social expectations and our educational structure have hardwired certain skills, practices and beliefs in us. We are using our hard-won skills every day. But is it time to outskill and be future-ready? We need to unlearn a few skills and relearn them in a new way. In the next section, we explore the traits that leaders will need to master in this changing landscape.

SECTION 2

Leadership Traits of the Future

The world has changed, and as humans we have a fascination—and a fear—for the kinds of technologies we believe will make human effort redundant. We romanticize it, for better or for worse, leading us to leap to the wrong conclusions. The reality is that none of us can know precisely what the future of work entails. But what we can say for certain is that machines will continue to get smarter and more capable of tasks we currently accept as our jobs. At the same time, the ways of working will change alongside the beliefs and needs of the future workforce.

We can't wait, watch and perish. Instead, we need to outskill and prepare ourselves for the future interconnected, virtual, corporate world. This preparedness can only come from openness, flexibility, adaptability and improved awareness, and from developing the skills our new world will demand of us.

I strongly believe that in life, everything starts with oneself. This is even more applicable if you are the type of person who likes to introspect, are open to change and are ready to make yourself a better individual.

In this fast-changing world, if you want to excel and reach the top, you have no choice but to dig deep to understand yourself.

Alvin Toffler once said: 'The illiterate of the twenty-first century will not be those who cannot read and write, but those who cannot learn, unlearn, and relearn.' I find this observation to be true in every sense. The funny part is that we are the ones inventing the technologies and designing the new processes that we then need to adapt to by continuously unlearning and relearning new skills in order to remain suitable for this new world of our own creation.

Most of these skills naturally will be about managing our virtual workspaces and embracing possibilities through technology. Other skills we will need in our arsenal might have more universal roots but call for a new kind of application.

Let us look at the leadership skills we foresee will change versus the way we are practising them today.

The first step is always about unlearning and relearning.

We have acquired our knowledge through years of education and experience. And that has helped us reach where we are today. We have achieved a degree of success with which we are either satisfied or dissatisfied. I am not talking about letting go of our hard-earned knowledge; I am talking about acquiring new knowledge and adapting to the new needs of society. Adaptability is key. The world today needs us to be a very different version of ourselves than we currently are. And this means we need to renew ourselves, unlearn many of our deep beliefs and embrace new ones.

It is our choice to change or not. But as most of us want to be successful, we need to remain relevant and adapt to changing technology and processes and how we deal with people.

These changes may make us feel insecure, but as I say, insecurity is the new security—it creates an appreciation for change and fosters the curiosity to explore and adapt to technology, processes and people. This shift is not easy without a conscious choice being made, till we decide for ourselves that we need to change and adapt to a new way to lead.

New-age leaders need to be on a path of continuous learning. We can start by identifying the gaps we have as leaders and acquiring new skills to help minimize those gaps. Unless we are aware of what is needed, we won't be able to carve out a road map to get there.

Technology

Let me start with a short story an Italian friend of mine once told me.

'Papa, when you were my age, what did you do on your holidays?' asked Graham, the fifteen-year-old son of George and Ana, while playing on his smartphone. They were at a beachside restaurant on the coast of Sicily during a family holiday in Italy.

George smiled. 'You might find my stories odd,' he said. 'We enjoyed playing volleyball on the beach, ran into the water on sunny days like this, and I had a great time talking to my father and hearing about his childhood stories. After all, we did not have smartphones in those days.'

Graham didn't pick up on the sarcasm in his dad's tone. 'We are so different, Papa.'

'Not really, life has moved on, and I understand the new generation's love for gadgets,' said George. 'Now imagine life further back, imagine the young days of your grandpa and grandma. Most of them did not even have a telephone, forget about the apps you are using today. Imagine a life that was all about face-to-face interactions and writing letters to one another. Do you know I wrote my parents a letter every week from my school hostel? How does that sound?'

'Funny,' replied Sarah, Graham's younger sister. 'I don't even want to know about those dark days.'

George shot his wife, Ana, a look. 'Those days were not dark, my lovely Sarah, and my parents survived and enjoyed their lives as well. But the truth is, we, as a society, are evolving fast.

The changes are hitting us faster than anticipated, and we are learning to live in a very different way.'

'And maybe twenty-five years down the line,' said Ana, 'when you are talking to your children, maybe at this same restaurant, they too will be surprised by your childhood. When you talk about the devices and technology you were using as you were growing up, don't be surprised if they laugh at you and feel sorry for you. Who knows, they might also feel that you had a dark childhood.'

Graham smiled. 'Come on, let's hit the water, it's 30 degrees out.'

This is a simple story, but I am sure you can relate to this conversation.

I remember when I was a child, waiting for the postman to deliver letters to our house. I now miss him as emails rule my life. In my apartment building, we had a liftman whose job it was to operate the lift and get us to our floor. He does not have a job anymore, either. My first CV was typed on an electronic typewriter by a typist. Today, computers are a part of life even in kindergarten. When I joined the corporate world, the office was full of large filing cabinets. Today we have moved towards paperless offices. I remember my first friend in my office was the telephone operator; that job does not exist anymore. When we went on holidays, we wrote letters or called the hotel to book a room; now we do it online. For my father, going to a bank to withdraw cash was a big deal; now we do it in minutes at an ATM or forego cash altogether in favour of digital payments. I could go on.

Coming back to my own function, finance, there are more specific examples. I have closed books of accounts, matched suppliers' bills with purchase orders and tracked customers' outstanding payments—all manually. Now it feels like a bad dream when I think of how much time I wasted on those tasks when today everything is automated. The financial analysis department no longer merely compiles data or generates reports; it tells the story behind the data. The role of a finance head is no longer considered to be that of a bean counter; instead, they are strategic advisors to CEOs. As a society, we have adapted to all these changes and progressed.

Today, the pace of change due to innovation has multiplied several times. Wherever we are, whoever we are, we can't shy away from these changes. I see even my mother at the age of eighty-nine learning to use WhatsApp to keep in touch with family that stays far away.

This is not a book about the specific technologies we need to learn—that will vary from person to person. The main point here is that we need to be in touch with change and adapt. We need to unlearn to learn many new things. We need to outskill ourselves to be ready for the next challenge.

People and process

I grew up in India and worked there for many years. The predominant style of leadership that I was accustomed to, and even admired, was mostly about command and control. It was simple: most of the time the leader would decide what was to be done, tell us to do it and we would execute and report back. I, being a movie addict, was drawn to the character of the 'boss', the one who decides, while his 'men or ladies' followed his orders. Such a simple life, was it not? The onus of failure and success was on the leader, while the only things I needed to worry about were dedication and hard work.

I have found that leadership styles have evolved globally. Nowadays, as a leader, you need to be much more inclusive and open rather than directional. Before, I saw many intuitive leaders who were extremely successful making decisions based on their instincts. Today, with the boom in technology, a leader is still needed to make the decisions and intuition is still a factor, but we are moving towards a much more balanced, inclusive landscape, backed by data.

Hierarchical leadership is a thing of the past. We need to lead our teams from the heart, to change our ways of communicating in the digital world, ensuring we remain connected mentally as we start working more remotely from each other. We need to learn to work in matrix organizations, to lead with self-efficacy, build emotional resilience and psychological safety, share success and failure through real-life stories, learn to coach and be coached. The rise of servant leadership will be eminent, where the main goal of leaders is to serve, quite different from hierarchical leadership. Such leaders will ensure that they share their powers, help their teams develop and perform better, and always put people first.

The whole process of dealing with problems is changing, which in turn, is affecting the way we lead and make decisions. When I joined the corporate world, leaders were treated as superheroes. They were our go-to people, the experts in most matters and treated as larger than life. We always looked up to them for advice. And to be honest, I was seldom disappointed as I was often able to find a solution with their guidance. They possessed much more knowledge and information than me, which made them special in my eyes.

With the digital world opening up, acquiring data and information is no longer the challenge. Instead, extracting meaning from data and information is what is expected from leaders. And that results in a continuous learning process. I do not remember my CEOs or CFOs or even senior leaders attending any training programmes, but today it is a common practice.

In this section of the book we will explore how a new-age leader can be mindful of and adapt to the new ways of working, based on the changes that are coming. We should not forget that all knowledge and experience is useful and hence, it is not about forgetting certain skills that we possess, but rather it is all about adding new traits to our kitty by keeping ourselves open to change. Who knows, one day we may need to relearn what we have just unlearnt!

UNLEARN/RELEARN VOICES

Manish Bhatia

'Leaders today are precisely the people who had never imagined that their academics would be irrelevant today, but by being on a self-learning curve, they have been able to not only command teams, but also command respect from peers and smart, next-level people with the latest education.'

Sarmila Basu

'The days of "command and control" culture are gone. In order to attract talent in today's competitive market, leaders have to be able to paint a compelling picture. Unless the leader is fairly data-driven and tech savvy, he/she will have a hard time leading today's workforce.

'While driving a mindset change in corporate culture and trying to bring people along, the leader needs to be highly adaptable. They need to practise "situational leadership" and not be rigid in their approach. We need to unlearn and relearn in many aspects.'

Arunabh Das Sharma

'An important skill for tomorrow is the ability to handle technology. You have to feel a little insecure about what you do because there is always somebody who is willing to work harder, who is smarter, perhaps younger, and who is willing to do it for much cheaper. That is why this can be a recipe for disaster when you're older, unless you decide to learn and adapt and have the ability to keep learning new things.

'Both the younger generation as well as the older generation should try to understand each other's perspectives and learn from them. Because in a group that consists of people of the same experience, everyone tends to think similarly. A kind of groupthink sets in. So you need to understand what the other generation is trying to do or say. It is all about unlearning, relearning and learning from each other.'

Ravi Sahgal

'Leaders need to unlearn and relearn to be customer-centric and less functional-centric, and remain open to new skills to fill in the knowledge gaps by self or collaboration. Leaders will be those who will be able to leverage the global ecosystem effectively instead of trying to build their own from scratch.'

Ashok Cherian

'Reskill or perish—I always believe in this mantra. It may sound dramatic, but it is true for all aspirants.

'For example, the digital challenge is as relevant in the C-suite as it is at other levels. Are our leaders ready to steer their companies smartly in the digital era? The answer found in many surveys is "no" for the majority. It's all about "digital IQ". Lack of skills, inflexibility and slow process are the top challenges for the C-suite, which need to be addressed. The leadership needs to acknowledge that what brought them to the current level is not going to take them to the next level and this is the most difficult challenge of unlearning at the C-level.'

Indraneel Roy Choudhury

'The view that the pandemic [is] more disruptive and devastating than anything one has experienced before has been stated by experts—the difference has been that all countries in the world are at war at the same time. This will mean different things to different countries, and the gap between the more developed and less developed ones will increase further. Technology adoption and upskilling are keeping us going in the new world. Here the next generation will have an edge over their elders as they have embraced this skill set in a much better way.'

Deepa Dey

'Being ready is about a set of things that you need to do— this is finite. The world has infinite opportunities, and we need to be open to unlearning and relearning as we jump into the brave new world. Our future leaders need to stay open to new learning, remain adaptable, swallow their egos as "subordinates" become teachers, work on their resilience as the speed at which things are changing will not allow for kindness to flourish. Remain curious, mentor, coach and train others. Enjoy the new learning.'

Himal Tiwari

'Constant upskilling will be the new way. The new drivers will be how quickly employees will learn and unlearn at the same time. This is the era of continuous learning—the learning will not stop at any level or age, and leaders will also have the humility to say that we don't know it all. The era of the narcissist leader will be challenged.'

Sanjesh Thakur

'Among the right set of qualities, the one that really tops the chart is what I call intellectual versatility. The reason is simple: the day-to-day challenges before any department of a company are no longer standard. The future leaders who can draw upon a broad range of experiences and are willing to unlearn and relearn will be the most successful. Long time back I heard someone say, "If you are not living on the edge, you are wasting space." In the new digital world of today, If you are not able to effectively utilize a multitude of data, you might be knocked off from the competitive landscape.'

Sunil Gupta

'What will always be relevant for managers is the ability to stay updated on the key levers of business and influence the same through the smart usage of evolving technologies and data analytics. People need to upskill and outskill.'

Soumen Mukherjee

'Careers are likely to be built in horizons of three to five years, where the new normal will not be a career switch, but a skill refresh. Those that are willing to invest in ceaseless learning and adaptation will acquire the skills to be continually relevant and successful.'

Dr P. V. Ramana Murthy

'Nandan Nilekani of Infosys once said that the old routine of learn-earn-retire needs to (and in many cases, already has) changed to learn-earn-relearn. Retirement is no longer a dead-end or a life event. One simply keeps engaged for as long as one can work, as long as one can unlearn and relearn.

'Being a perennial student is the core trait that will allow us to develop all the others we will need as we move ahead. Let us now take a closer look at the specific skills we need to hone, starting with what it means to lead virtually.'

Puneet Gupta

'Gone are the days of holding authority, information and decisions. We are entering a different phase where openness is going to be up there for all. Power shall not be drawn from keeping information close to your heart but from sharing it. There will be a paradigm shift and one of the toughest ones today's leaders shall have to encounter. Passion will climb right to the top as the most important metric for success.'

3

Virtual Leadership

Many professionals wonder if it is really that different to lead virtually. My answer is yes, it is very different from leading a team sharing the same office space as you.

While the trend has been evolving over the years, with teams going global and remote, the need to master this leadership skill has come into sharp focus due to the onset of the COVID-19 pandemic. Lockdowns have forced people to work remotely, and leaders to lead virtually. Some have sailed unperturbed through these new waters. Others, unprepared for such change, have sunk. These people had perhaps assumed that the usual ways of interaction would never change, that they would always be able to continue with their 'in person' leadership style. And then they were proven wrong.

In traditional leadership, personal relations play a big role. I know some leaders claim their success relies on 'MDWA' (managing by walking around). Some say it's all about personal attention and being with the team. There's nothing wrong with any of these styles in themselves. But in the digital age, many such walks or meetings have been converted into virtual interactions, which calls for a different way of conducting oneself as a leader. With teams spreading across the globe, leaders aren't able to supervise their teams with direct one-on-one contact. This fundamental change will be further enabled by technological advances that will make the interactions seamless. The future will see very different ways of talking and interacting.

Sam, a good friend of mine, leads the marketing function for a global confectionary manufacturer based in Zurich. He has a small central team and there are regional heads too who report remotely.

Sam's job involves designing the strategic framework for his function as well as managing the delivery of regular operational tasks. Over time, it became more and more difficult to manage both fronts, and since the CEO wanted Sam to spend more time defining strategy for the organization, the company decided to appoint a head of marketing operations under Sam with the hope that moving forward, Sam would be able to focus on marketing strategies while also keeping an eye on the operations side.

Sam had two options—to look outside the organization and recruit someone who had run such a massive operation before, or to promote one of the regional heads and fill the position internally. Sam decided to promote an internal talent and offered the job to the regional head of Latin America, Rodrigo—the senior most and undoubtedly the brightest.

In a few months, however, it became clear that Rodrigo was not the right person for the role. He failed to deliver. Sam kept working with Rodrigo, but matters did not improve. To cut a long story short, it was a bad decision and eventually Rodrigo decided to leave the organization and go back to Brazil.

After a few months, Sam called me as he was still upset with himself for not being able to make Rodrigo successful. We analysed every move that Rodrigo had made while leading the team and finally agreed that while he might have been a great manager in a traditional set-up with his teams around him, he was not ready for virtual leadership. And Sam, as his manager, had missed the need to make him 'virtually ready'. The result was a great talent loss for the company.

Following are a few tips on how we can lead virtually with greater effectiveness.

Demonstrate trust

Trust plays an even bigger role in virtual leadership as the leader and teams are separated geographically. The team should never wonder if their leaders trust them to deliver on time as committed. This should be the foundation of a relationship for better understanding and mutual respect, with clear expectations for delivery.

Be present

As a leader, you need to pour your heart and mind into any meeting or interaction that you lead virtually. Those on the other side can clearly sense if you are present, listening and contributing. Every silence or every word spoken is amplified a thousand times and people feel the commitment and mood clearly. If they feel you are not present, your team won't be there for you either. Prepare carefully for every interaction: we know that poor preparation never helps, be it for a virtual or face-to-face meeting.

Every individual may need different ways to be dealt with

Virtual leadership requires the leader to put in extra effort to know each member of the team well, to understand their individual needs and motivations. The needs and ways of working may vary for different individuals due to cultural differences, geographical situations or because of the stage of life a person is in. Without knowing each other well, virtual leadership may lead to mechanical interactions, which may not bring about the best results.

Make expectations clear

Ambiguity never helps, especially when the interaction is virtual. When the teams are in the same physical space, if something is vague, you can easily clarify it. But virtually, it takes much more effort. Clear expectations help avoid loss of efficiency and productivity and stave off any disengagement or demotivation. Ensure that the team knows what success looks like and how its performance will be measured and evaluated.

Establish structural governance, reviews and follow-ups

With teams being spread out, chances of informal discussions in the hallway or in the coffee corner are fewer. A clear governance calendar with pre-planned meetings is essential for virtual leadership as it helps communicate the discipline you would like to follow and grabs attention in advance. Avoid last-minute invites whenever possible.

Let go but provide support

Much of the time, virtual leadership means people are left alone in their country or region to act on their own. This means you need to let go of many decisions, leaving them to the team's judgement within the framework defined. However, as a leader, you need to understand the support your team requires to deliver a task and provide it to them. In some cases, the support expected may be minimal, but even so, listening and acknowledging their challenges and honestly working towards a solution drives stronger performance. It will also help adjust the direction of the sails in case course correction is required.

Celebrate

Celebrate every way you can, recognize each other's effort and keep appreciating, acknowledging and cheering about it. Even a virtual pat on the back can do wonders. We often forget to celebrate as we lead from a distance since, many a time, we link celebration to a dinner or drinking session. That's a myth, I would argue. Just learn to celebrate.

VIRTUAL LEADERSHIP VOICES

Gopi Koteeswaran

'In addition to reading a physical room, learning how to read a virtual room will be critical to assess the social mood across the organization.'

Sandeep Batra

'Gone are the days when all our teams used to be physically around us. Now you may not meet your team in weeks or months. So how do you motivate them? Connecting with them is a key issue.'

Syed Safawi

'Managing in a tech-enabled, data-driven, impersonal, multi-location environment will be the most significant leadership challenge ... How to maximize human potential in this work environment is a question for all future leaders.'

Dhiren Kinger

'Virtual skills, with the ability to be sensitive to cultures and people without fully knowing them, will be of tremendous help for future leaders. We all need to master this trait.'

Ashish Aul

'In this era of AI and automation, we need to embrace technology in our ways of working and constantly upgrade ourselves, but I still believe that it should not replace the human touch. I believe that specially during these challenging and turbulent times, leaders need to find ways of connecting with teams and constantly build trust, and connect more regularly in groups as well as one-on-one. Leading teams virtually won't be the same.'

Now let us look at how the virtual world and technology are moving us towards matrix organizations and how we need to be different in order to excel in those environments.

4

Matrix Leadership

During the first few years of my corporate journey, I was exposed to traditional hierarchical management layers. My exposure to the matrix way of working happened once I became part of a global team based in Amsterdam. The matrix model is a great way to foster collaboration among cross-functional teams as it helps break down silos, which is a prevalent problem for many hierarchical organizations.

Let me first define what I mean by 'matrix organization'. In simple terms, it means one person is part of cross-functional teams with shared objectives and may thus have more than one reporting manager. As per its definition, a matrix has a horizontal and a vertical axis, and balancing both is critical. It is not about creating more jobs for one person, but rather it is about harnessing the capability of an organization by bringing more resources together to ensure success. It's a new trend and an important one to facilitate agile leadership, which we will address in another chapter.

The trend is clear—organizations are adopting the new model, but it has not been easy for them to move towards this structure, since the skills required to work in a matrix organization are different from those it takes to succeed in the typical hierarchical models, and many organizations and professionals are not ready for these new ways of working. The workforce still needs to adapt.

Let us first talk about the skills we need to work in a matrix organization.

Influencing

In hierarchical organizations, one-on-one manager–employee relationships help steer the course. In matrix organizations, however, we deal with people who do not fall in our direct line of management. The ability to influence others is thus an essential skill, as many a time, you need to build consensus in cross-functional teams, and you may find yourself leading though you are not the boss.

Listening

This is a basic and probably one of the most important skills needed to be successful in a matrix organization. With a criss-crossing hierarchical structure and cross-functional relations, one needs to listen even more carefully to understand and appreciate other viewpoints. Mistrust and silo thinking start when people feel that they are unable to communicate their thoughts to others, and that can only be resolved by deep listening.

Being open

Everyone has unique strengths, and all those strengths collectively become the power of a matrix organization. Hence, you should be clear about what strengths you bring to the team as well as about the areas in which you need help. This will help the team know each other better and come forward with complementary skills to ensure success.

Teamwork

Matrix organizations are all about shared delivery, and teamwork is extremely important. People who are used to individualistic delivery need to get used to working in a team and working for a team. Empathy will become even more important as understanding other perspectives is critical for a team to succeed.

Conflict management

Conflict is bound to arise when people from diverse backgrounds, with ambiguously defined authority lines, work together. Learning to manage conflict helps one to be more effective in such an environment.

One learning that I received when I was training to become a professional coach is QTIP: quit taking it personally. This simple thought helps me remain calm and not react when I do not like something; instead, I try to understand the motive and meaning behind it. This helps me avoid conflict.

Commitment to delivery

Working in a matrix organization requires a commitment to deliver, on time and in full, since it is not about individual delivery, but rather collective delivery. As in a relay race where you need to pass the baton to the next person to get to the finish line, here too the completion of your tasks is often crucial for others to succeed.

Here is a story that illustrates how, if not handled properly, matrix organizations can lead to utter confusion.

Anurag was an analyst at an airline, reporting to the head of financial reporting and analysis. The company had been growing well in terms of revenue and fleet size, but was making substantial losses, which were draining cash faster than expected. Anurag, being part of the finance team, saw the need to change the pricing or cost structure to generate more cash, else the airline would soon go bankrupt.

The company appointed a new CFO, who came from a new-age e-commerce company and was known for his pragmatic approach to resolving issues and handling crises. Upon joining, he promoted the idea of cross-functional teams and a matrix reporting structure. A task force was formed to draw up a turnaround strategy headed by the chief operating officer (COO), and the team had participation from all relevant functions. As a result, reporting lines were changed and Anurag had to report to two managers, and his second manager was the COO leading the task force.

The team had about ten high-potential members and started working with a ton of energy. However, in a few weeks, four of them reported in sick and stopped coming in to work. The project slowed down. New members were added to the team and the project continued. The following week, two other members resigned, including Anurag.

The CFO was worried and wanted to know the real reason behind the resignations. He knew Anurag well from a past association with him and decided to have a conversation with him. That was when Anurag opened up about his real reason for leaving: the confusion around what was expected of him. He said that his direct manager and the COO had each given different directions regarding the purpose of the team. While his direct manager was more concerned about the loss of profitability and loss of cash, the COO wanted to focus on operating efficiency and was pushing more flights per day even in sectors where they were making substantial losses.

The conversation enabled the CFO to gain a fair understanding of how the team was operating, and he was able to retain Anurag by promising him that the team's way of working would change, and he would ensure the implementation of a proper matrix structure.

We just read about Anurag, and how the CFO needed to step in to salvage the situation. Here are few points we should keep in mind when implementing a matrix structure.

Define expectations

Remove any ambiguity for the team. Once it is clear what success looks like, delivery will be smoother. Do not leave anything to chance or guesswork; define clear responsibilities and accountabilities through a RACI (responsible, accountable, consulted, informed) chart.

Create a safe environment

This is a key job for a leader. A safe environment helps people contribute freely and give their best (as we will explore in depth in the section on psychological safety). In a hierarchical organization, it is much easier to sort out misconceptions or delivery challenges through one-on-one conversations. In a matrix set-up, everyone needs to feel even safer than in a traditional one to avoid confusion and missteps.

Build a diverse team

A team with complementary skills will thrive in such an environment. Choose matrix relations carefully and ensure that the team has a balance of all the skills it needs. Diversity helps create a more rounded point of view and is critical for such a team to excel.

Foster structured communication

Communication is the key for such organizations to succeed. Hence, clearly define governance and meeting calendars, and ensure discipline is maintained in following those calendars. If that means over-communication and more frequent reviews for some time till the team starts delivering, then so be it.

Abolish silo culture

Since people from different departments will be working together, one of the important factors for success is breaking down silos and ensuring the team has a common objective. It requires constant counselling and coaching by the leader to ensure that the team understands why they are together, why they need to address some greater objective for the organization, and that this objective can't be achieved through a silo approach.

Support development

A few members will need to develop some skills to be effective in the new set-up, and as a leader, you need to ensure you help them with the required training and development. New competencies will be required, and a proper skill-gap analysis backed by a sound programme will be key to success.

Embrace failure

Failure is part of any change, and to accomplish such a great change, you will need to accept failure sometimes. But aborting such a transformational journey midway due to a few glitches is only a path backwards. Allow time for the team to adjust, build confidence among the members and provide opportunities for them to find their own solutions, rather than going into escalation mode to have issues solved by someone senior.

Deal with emotions

In a non-hierarchical organization, conflict is bound to occur. This may lead to team members expressing emotions that some might consider uncomfortable in the workplace. But emotions need not be destructive; I always argue that people who show emotion are good for an organization as they are passionate about winning.

MATRIX LEADERSHIP VOICES

Vineet Kapila

'With increasing number of young talent joining the industry every year, the more experienced professionals have to remain relevant to the newcomers. Hierarchies and authorities will be a thing of the past while transparency and collaboration in a digital world will lead the new way of working. I could well be working on a worksheet being in one part of the world, and have my co-worker sitting in another hemisphere to collaborate with and work together with me. The senior leaders will have to go back to being individual contributors again. While we all strive to deliver great outcomes, the fear is that with disaggregated teams, work-from-home culture and matrix organizations, the leaders need to encourage self-drive and discipline.'

Subroto Gupta

'Focus on creating diverse teams—diversity of background, skills and viewpoints. Unfortunately, diversity has increasingly become synonymous with gender, which is a fundamentally flawed view. And inclusivity has perceptual linkages to different forms of disability. Future leaders need to be able to actively encourage the formation of teams, which bring together people of different backgrounds, skills, personalities and viewpoints. This diversity will encourage the identification of new and innovative solutions, and complementary skill sets will ensure better execution and impact.

'We also need humility to accept that hierarchy does not equate to better knowledge and understanding. For much of modern history, knowledge has been distributed based on hierarchy and there existed a significant gap in the information available to different groups within an organizational or social structure. With a vast percentage of the information today going online and many available tools making the aggregation and search for it effortless, access to information is now democratized. Therefore, the differentiation for leaders is going to depend less on knowing all the data and facts and more on the ability to listen to the ideas and opinions of others. Leading in matrix organizations will be so different.'

Kiran Koteshwar

'Adaptability and effective communication will be some of the key traits of future. We need to shed our old mindsets and encourage collaborations instead of being hierarchical. As leaders, we need to stay tuned and be watchful of the changes around us.'

Pranesh Chatterjee

'Typical hierarchical organizations may cease to exist; rather people will prefer to work more in matrix-like organizations. In fact, fewer levels of management will be preferred to reduce costs, bureaucracy, time of execution and inefficiency in decision-making. There will be no "top-down" approach, no imposition. A collaborative environment will be encouraged in all management practices.

'Moving forward, organizations will have to increase acknowledgement—to know how to appreciate people in an unprejudiced and genuine way and encourage a collaborative environment. They will have to create a feeling of "ownership" amongst all employees.'

Sarmila Basu

'Leaders need to be innovative, a lot more so in today's world. As we see huge changes in technology around us as well as changes in the workforce, how we work is also changing. As a result, collaboration and cross-domain partnership is increasing. Leaders will need to be able to harness this opportunity to create innovative solutions in anticipation of a customer's needs.'

Both virtual and matrix working will need leaders who can thrive in an environment even where they are not the boss. Let us look at informal leadership, in other words, leading without title and connecting with others.

5

Be the Connector

We just read about how organizations are moving towards a matrix structure, and how the picture of a typical organization's structure with a straight boss-subordinate relationship will become less common. The future of leadership will not be based on position and power. A true leader will be the one who can connect others, leads irrespective of his or her position and is able to provide direction to and influence a group of people, be it the peers, juniors or even seniors, to move ahead, even when he or she doesn't have any direct authority over them.

Success will be determined by demonstrating clear leadership, by taking risks, displaying thought leadership while listening to others and carrying the team along. The leader is the person who makes everyone feel comfortable yet holds them accountable, is able to effectively engage one and all, ensures a review mechanism and provides constructive feedback—while everyone wins together. However, this does not mean all hierarchy in the corporate world will vanish. What we are talking about is informal leadership, where people will lead even without a crown on their heads and being named the boss.

Let me tell you about Johana, a young graduate, whom I met a few years back. Those days I was pursuing a certification to become a professional coach, and as part of my study assignment, I needed to coach someone who is fresh into the corporate world. I requested Johana to help me and she agreed.

The first thing I noticed about Johana was her confidence and willingness to take up challenges. We had several conversations as I coached her on different topics. One day, she was extremely happy and excited and told me that she had been promoted to lead a team of forty people. Never before in her organization had a young graduate with just three years of experience been given such a huge responsibility. She explained why she felt she had gotten the break. The following is her account:

'I was part of the project team that was leading transformation for the marketing function. I got the opportunity as my manager thought I would be able to put stories into great PowerPoint presentations, and the progress of the project required someone to put information together to be presented to senior management.

'I felt grateful to my manager as it was indeed a great opportunity for me to learn. Unfortunately, my manager, who was leading the transformation, had an accident and had to go on leave for a few months. We were told to continue with our tasks and that the manager would lead us remotely once he got a little better.

'Over time, I realized we were not progressing, and the project had almost come to a standstill. The team missed a leader.

'I decided to give it a try. I started organizing meetings where wo agrood on tho noīt otopo, roporting progrooo in a way that my manager would have done. At the first few meetings, people ignored me, but I was persistent. To change their mindset, and make them serious about their delivery, I scheduled review meetings with senior management and let the team know about it. Now there was no option but to progress. People were upset with me as I took that step despite being the junior-most in the team. I assured them that I would take the lead to ensure the tasks were divided and progress tracked.

'Over time, people started showing me respect, and I started believing in myself as a leader representing my manager. And we, as a team, delivered the transformation programme.

Soon after that, I got a call from my manager about my promotion.'

The following are a few tips on informal leadership qualities that I learnt from Johana's story.

Facilitate decision-making

One of the top expectations from a leader is that he or she should not be afraid to take decisions. In a situation where there is no defined leadership hierarchy, a person will be deemed a leader when he or she is able to facilitate discussions in such a way that the group can arrive at a decision.

Align on clear goals and gain commitments

It is true that a team with a clear objective and goal in mind will achieve better, more measurable results, than one with ambiguous targets. Thus, to establish oneself as a leader, it is important to agree on clear goals for the team and ensure that accountability is well defined and accepted by each member.

Create an environment to participate

A culture that collaborates and co-creates is always more effective than an individualistic culture. One needs to foster a culture where everyone is heard, every opinion is considered. A culture of openness fosters creativity and can inspire ordinary teams to deliver extraordinary results, and a person who can facilitate that culture will be accepted as a natural leader.

Maintain relationships

In times when formal leadership is missing, a good network can help overcome bottlenecks. Often, knowing the right people comes in handy. Thus, networking in a digital world will be an important trait to master (addressed later in the book).

Demonstrate thought leadership

People look to those who demonstrate thought leadership. To achieve this, it is important for a leader to be knowledgeable beyond his or her area of expertise, and to know people or organizations that can provide such expertise. Do not just remain a subject-matter expert; explore beyond your regular area of work. A thought leader provides energy to the team through common sense, innovative ideas and innovative ways to accomplish a task.

Establish a review process

It is important that a diligent review mechanism be established. Setting up clear deliverables, agreeing on a team charter, review calendar and governance structure will help the leader establish himself/herself within the team and drive progress effectively.

Resolve conflicts

Any team with diverse interests and without a formal leader is prone to experiencing conflict. A leader will be a person who can remain calm as emotions flow and convert them into fact-based actions. He or she needs to understand the root cause of the conflict and effectively guide the team towards a solution.

Be humble

There can be a tendency to become arrogant when a group appoints you as a leader, even when the stated corporate hierarchy does not do so. A person will continue to lead effectively if he or she can demonstrate humility. There is a fine line between arrogance and confidence, and a leader needs to understand where that lies.

BE THE CONNECTOR VOICES

Prabal Mitra

'Leaders will need to be more open, humble and authentic than ever before. Servant leadership will gain more and more strength as the workforce becomes laden with the younger generation that will not defer to power and authority, but will walk an extra mile for a unified purpose.'

Subroto Gupta

'Skill sets and not titles will increasingly define your identity; learning will be more modular and contextual. You need to be the connector.'

Jayesh Desai

'A key consequence of the earlier industrial revolutions has been the increasing role of middle management. The current revolution will, in all likelihood, reverse the trend. Jobs will continue to exist at the lower levels and more and more jobs will be created at the top for people who can work with artificial intelligence, possess analytical skills and are high on people skills. Many supervisory jobs will disappear and the concept of "span of control" will lose relevance. However, even in areas where there is more middle management, the role of the middle manager will disappear and one will increasingly see either front-facing people or analysts interacting directly with each other, or with machines rather than having a coordinator and supervisor.'

Puneet Gupta

'It is expected that a senior lead should have deep understanding about how different functions in an organization work. To knit the organization together and to make them dream big, the leader needs to have empathy and understanding of various roles/functions. For example, to be a leader who is a great connector— no matter how brilliant you are in your functions like, say, supply chain or finance—unless you are a consumer/market savvy, you won't be successful. You need to know more than your job description.'

Nihil Dey

'Building a team that is geared to forget its territorial mindset and collaborate seamlessly across geographies, and with other partners of a client, will be truly value-additive. Leaders, be they formal or informal, need to invest in promoting a collaborative approach, which will become a core part of what it takes to succeed.'

Shridhar Narayan

'Leadership has been studied extensively and classified into many styles: autocratic, democratic, servant, disruptive, and so on. In today's disruptive world, is one single style still effective? An entirely new value system is beginning to emerge for the leaders of the future, and that will continue to grow with the rise of new tools like artificial intelligence, robotics, 3D printing and automation. These technological advances are already disrupting almost every industry, and to master this new digital world, leaders must be agile and have an adaptive style. The old hierarchical model that depended mostly on a few people at the top for leadership will not work anymore. Going forward, an informal leadership style will be imperative for success.'

Informal and virtual leadership, when supported by stories, can become deeper and more connected. Let us look at the need for storytelling in the future world.

6

Lead through Stories

When I was a child, every night before bed, my mother would tell me a new tale. I loved all her stories. I always wondered how she had such a vast repertoire, and it was only much later that I realized that she used to draw those stories from her real life. They touched me so much and were so close to life that I still remember them.

We all go through many leadership courses, hear a lot of jargon from management gurus and learn different leadership styles and techniques. In reality, most of the time we forget the outcome within days unless we relate to it and the learning resonates with us.

In my view, what sticks are those little stories that float all around us. When we think of countries around the world, we look for the stories that shaped their cultures. Every story tells us something about that society and its history, culture, people, food and beliefs, but interestingly, the way each person absorbs the learnings from stories depends on his or her values, upbringing, stage of life, mental state and more.

Till recently, this skill of storytelling has been largely ignored in the corporate world as a leadership trait. However, organizations have now realized that stories are a powerful communication tool that can be used to motivate employees and convey messages effectively instead of shoving them down our throats. This is not a trait that every leader today has acquired; most of us have to learn this skill.

Stories can be simple and come from life experience. The important part is mastering the skill of connecting with others to drive home a point.

As leaders, we need to be mindful of the relevance of a story and how it is linked to the objective we want to achieve. The stories need not come from CEOs or CXOs, anyone at any level can be a storyteller and can effect change. Stories help leaders to lead their employees towards a vision by relating to an actual situation and can be a great tool to drive an objective, lead transformation, inspire teams or define cultures.

Many companies are now promoting storytelling as a corporate function as part of their communication strategy, and they have designated people to do that. Some organizations are still thinking about how to embed this new need into their managers' capabilities and are encouraging their employees to embrace this skill. It is time for us all to hone this skill.

Below are a few tips for effective storytelling.

Choose a story you are convinced about

If you can choose a story from your life or something you have experienced or heard about yourself, you will be most convincing. The closer you are to the story, the more relatable it will be for your audience. It is important that the storyteller is convinced about what he or she is talking about and believes in the story to ensure it also resonates with the listeners. A fake story never works.

Be inspired, not literal

We all need to respect the privacy of others as we share stories. It is not about avoiding legal issues, it is also about respecting others as many stories are personal in nature and the subjects may not like them to be shared. Avoid such stories or tweak and rewrite them keeping the learning intact. When I need to share an actual incident or quote names, I ensure I seek permission. So take the kernel of a story and adapt it to your needs, changing the specifics.

Define the context carefully

I have seen storytellers start abruptly without giving the context for what they would like to communicate. This does not work. Ensure that you define the context in a way that people understand where you are heading with your story. That way you can create anticipation in your audience.

Keep it short and to the point

Time is precious, people are not there to listen to your story just for the sake of it—you are using your story to drive home a point. Keep it short, focused, and most importantly, relevant.

Keep it relatable

Great storytellers use metaphors or anecdotes that anyone can relate to, cutting across cultures and geographies.

Respect the culture of the organization and audience

Every organization or geography has its own culture, and one needs to understand that. Some stories are acceptable in one culture or country but are a no-no in another.

Use humour carefully

Humour, I always say, is a double-edged sword. It also differs from culture to culture. I sometimes do not understand or laugh at a joke or a statement even though I can see others enjoying it. If your audience doesn't understand your humour, it can backfire. So be cautious.

Use emotions and voice modulation

If you want to make an impact on people's minds and hearts, you need to be an actor while narrating a story. A monologue delivered in a flat tone will never reach your audience. They should feel the emotion while you narrate your story. Some training and practise will certainly help.

Get your audience involved

Pause where required, ask for acknowledgement, feel the pulse of the audience. Or else your story won't reach your listeners.

While I have many stories to share about the power of storytelling, let me tell you one from my airline days.

For any airline, one of the largest costs is fuel, and it is a cost that airlines have no direct control over. A few years ago, when the price of crude oil was at its highest, airlines had to look at other opportunities to cut costs or increase revenue in order to survive. As increasing revenue was not that easy an option due to cut-throat competition in the market, the airlines had to look inwards to cut costs.

At this time, one of the airlines was selling about ten million seats per annum. While analysts had warned the airline about the rising crude prices, somehow the message had not landed across the organization. Despite repeated reminders, the employees were not taking the message seriously that they needed to save costs in order to survive.

The CEO passed on the task of changing this attitude to the CFO, who then called for an all-employee meeting. During this interaction, he shared a story he had heard from his father a long time ago.

'It was during World War II; my grandfather was then working for a paint manufacturer. While the need for infrastructural material was high in order to rebuild nations, the competition for and cost of raw materials were also quite high. My grandfather was the manufacturing head of a plant that produced about 2,00,000 cans of paint a year. It was clear to him that they needed to cut costs in order to remain profitable, and he proposed to save 50 cents per can. It was an easy target, and his colleagues agreed. Each department then divided the target among themselves, which was quite achievable.'

The CFO then looked around the room. 'Can you tell me what they achieved by saving that mere 50 cents?' he asked one of young employees in the audience.

'Together they achieved a reduction of EUR 1,00,000 per annum,' he replied.

The CFO smiled. 'How simple yet innovative is that?'

'But why is this story relevant to us?' asked another member of the audience.

'Our average cost of ticket is about EUR 50. Can we save just 2 per cent, by which I mean EUR 1, per passenger?' the CFO asked.

'Yes we can, but how does that help?' they wondered.

'Do you know the value of that EUR 1 to the company? It means 10 million to our cash flow and bottom line, since we fly about 10 million passengers a year.'

It was such a powerful message, delivered through a story. Everyone agreed to save just EUR 1 per passenger, and the company benefitted by EUR 10 million.

The next day, the CFO framed a few EUR 1 coins and wrote EUR 1 = EUR 10 million. They were shipped to various airports and all the airline's offices for display, where they served as a reminder of the commitment they had all made. And around the world, the entire team delivered.

This is the power of storytelling.

LEAD THROUGH STORIES VOICES

Monideepa Bhattacharya

'Storytelling is a skill and an art. I was struggling, in the early COVID-19 days, to even understand the actual implications of this virus. There just seemed to be too many sources for information, too much choice, issues with veracity, sensationalism and too many ways of telling the same story, and it was still not clear.

'But then, some stories began to stick. The famous "flatten the curve" visual that finally made people change their individual behaviour and the "hand washing" ad on Tiktok that got fifty billion views are examples of powerful stories that have universal appeal and change mass behaviour.

'We all need to be better storytellers—to change behaviours, to sell, to empathize, to make sense of data. There is a greater need than ever to be able to "connect"—the human touch is possibly reducing or changing in texture and the only way we can re-establish personal and professional relationships within the boundaries necessary is through powerful stories.'

Shyam Mamidi

'In the new era, storytelling will be an important feature. One example of this is in customer journey mapping, where mapping the impacts on clients down the chain and all the way up to the end consumer will impact our understanding of how one's products and offerings should be fine-tuned repeatedly to create a unique customer experience.'

Sreenivasa Rao Yadavilli

'Humans will always tell stories—how they do this is what will change. If earlier the boss told stories over a beer after work, it will move to social media and become folklore in a new way.'

Surajit Banerjee

'Storytelling is an easy way to assimilate narrative styles. Not all professionals are comfortable or proficient using this. However, a good alternative could be illustrative dashboards and case simulations.'

Anushree Singh

'Storytelling is an important trait, especially in leadership communication. When professionals bring realism and authenticity and don't refrain from sharing their vulnerability in their communication, storytelling will become their natural style. It is simple yet powerful and transformational.'

Ramanan G.V.

'The ability to communicate simply and succinctly is an important trait that holds good even in the post-COVID-19 world. As digital transformation gains more speed, the workforce in companies will be more visible, and hence it is important for HR learning teams to focus on this—to help leaders get more comfortable with this change.'

Subodh Dubey

'Storytelling is a common technique which helps leaders connect with their teams and makes it easier to get a task done. It is easy to manage people and get your work done with this technique. Professionals can embed stories by using their own experiences, adding some surprise and conflict and by telling stories as they do in their day-to-day lives.'

Prriti Narain

'A powerful personal narrative immediately forms a connection with your audience. Authentic, data-backed and succinct stories help relate to the audience. Leaders and managers who feel comfortable with this style can embrace this to create a compelling shared vision.'

Prabal Mitra

'One of the top qualities will be storytelling capabilities. A leader who can draw observations from life and convert these into relatable stories to drive home a point will be regarded well in the future.'

Dilip Pal

'Storytelling will be one of the most powerful means for leaders to influence, teach and inspire teammates. Storytelling builds connections among people. COVID-19 is showing us an entirely new way of living, managing self and managing teams. Team members constantly need to know what's going on. With work-from-home, team members feel they have been separated from the mothership and social distancing measures mean they are missing human connection. Leaders with a powerful storytelling trait will be able to communicate and engage employees by sharing stories of success and failure, stories of exceptional heroics in managing crises, showing them the purpose of the company and what they stand for.'

While storytelling is all about observation, connecting the dots and a creative mind, nursing that creativity will be another important task for the future leader. Let's take a closer look.

7

Harness Creativity

I strongly believe each one of us is creative in one way or another; however, most of us keep our creativity suppressed. A creative mind is always needed and appreciated in the corporate world and has always been a tool for the start of a revolution or to outshine competition.

Everyday, new challenges and opportunities are thrown at us; they can come from any direction. Leaders have realized that creativity cannot be left to a set of people who are known as innovators; creativity is needed in our day-to-day life and work and needs to be fulfilled by each of us. It is not always about a big innovation; it can also be about little tweaks. Every mind needs to think out of the box.

Today, many corporate executives feel there is too much to do and too little time. Thus, for many of us, creative thinking takes a backseat as we get busy with the problems of today and have no time for those of tomorrow. But in order to stay ahead of the curve by remaining relevant to the market and to society, an organization needs to ensure that its people are encouraged to remain creative and are not spending all their time on execution. The new workforce is also looking for a culture where it can contribute to the future, and this calls for a cultural change in many organizations. If we don't move to meet these needs, we will be living in the past while the world will move on to the future.

I met Tisham on a flight last year, when I was travelling between New Delhi and Mumbai. She holds a doctorate in biochemistry and works as a research scientist for a pharmaceutical company.

This is Tisham's story:

'I have a passion for developing apps. While I have no formal education in computer science, I learnt out of curiosity in my spare time. I get energy from solving issues through those apps.

'In a townhall a few years back, our CEO told us he would like each employee to visit the retailers and distributors to help us develop an understanding of how we conduct our business. He wanted feedback from us in order to improve our products and services.

'I liked the idea and started travelling to markets close to my house. In a few weeks, I gained so much knowledge that my interest grew and every weekend, I started visiting new markets.

'While talking to the retailers, I realized that most of them struggle with tracking the expiry dates of medicines. While most of them have a tracker installed on their computers, which tracks expiry dates for stock they are carrying, they felt it was not adequate to keep tight control and that they were losing money as a result. The company policy stated that expired medicines could be returned within seven working days for a 50 per cent refund. But if the return occurred after this, the amount dropped to 25 per cent.

'At most retailers, the computer system was handled not by the owner but by an employee. The owners wanted to control this issue themselves and were looking for a simple reminder on their cell phones that they could track easily.

'The retailers claimed that they had raised this issue with the sales managers but had not seen much progress so far.

'Over the next few weeks, I went on to develop an app which would link their system and their phone, allowing them to scroll through the list of expired medicines and the dates by which they would need to be returned to meet the seven-day criteria. I tested the app with a few retailers, and it worked well. They all wanted the app installed, but I knew it would have to be rolled out by the sales team after due testing by our information technology department.

'I spoke to my manager who was highly pleased with my innovation, and he got me an appointment with the CEO and the CIO the very next week. I explained the features with live data, and our CEO wanted the app to be tested and rolled out.

'Today, my app is used across the country. Our CEO has spread the word across the organization about how we should never be restrictive in our own function as creativity has no limit.

'My story encouraged many youngsters to come forward with their ideas. I am now part of the creativity board, and every week, we evaluate new ideas flowing in from across the country. I am surprised at the brain power we have in our organization!

'Since our organization motivates people to be creative and has a clear process to ensure all ideas go through proper evaluation, to me it feels like I am working here to be rewarded for my passion, and this helps me sail through all the hard work I take on.'

Below are a few learnings from Tisham's story.

Encourage imagination

Great strategy and proper execution are the keys to success, we all know that. But that should not stop us from encouraging our organizations to imagine new possibilities through creative thinking, what we popularly call 'out-of-the-box thinking'. Not many leaders are comfortable encouraging imagination, but while some ideas may indeed sound out of place and might feel like a waste of time, encouraging imagination is never a bad idea.

Create a culture to contribute

We cannot expect all great ideas to come from senior leaders. There will be people way down in the hierarchy who are creative and full of ideas. We need to ensure we reach out to them, encourage them to contribute and then capture their ideas for evaluation. More contributors enhance the chances of success.

Diversity matters

Diversity breeds creativity. The more diverse our teams are in terms of gender, culture, location and expertise, the more likely they are to be creative. As leaders, we need to engage different minds in the same team to broaden horizons. The virtual world has brought us even closer in a sense, with location no longer acting as a constraint to assembling diverse teams to work together, even if they are far apart.

Acknowledge and reward

No one knows how an idea can change the dynamic and future of an organization. While we need to reward great ideas, even acknowledging ideas that are not adopted can help build a creative culture in the organization. Leaders need to be mindful of this simple step. A good leader needs to be part of the process to inspire through acknowledgement and reward as needed. When a leader hampers this process, perhaps through neglect, it will negatively impact employee morale.

Define a process to nurture ideas

Too many processes are believed to kill creativity. However, process-based organizations can facilitate creativity by nurturing ideas into action. Often, the original idea can get lost as it passes through different stages towards finalization, mostly due to organization hierarchical influence, bias or bureaucracy, and a leader needs to protect against such deviation. A clear process can also help screen ideas and not leave the filtering to bias or organizational politics. The leaders need to ensure the right people are involved: those who can understand and appreciate ideas and are committed to taking them to the next level. Shepherding ideas should not be left to those with no appreciation for innovation.

Accept failure

Even after going through all processes and stage-gates, some ideas will fail. Leaders need to make sure they create an environment to accept such failures and that there is no mudslinging or blame-game. People need to feel psychologically safe and not fear failure if we want to encourage creativity.

HARNESS CREATIVITY VOICES

Surajit Banerjee

'The digital and virtual world have set every working person physically free, to work independently in their space with a loose thread monitoring performance delivery. This throws up constantly changing scenarios requiring new ways of doing things. The days of common organizational workflows are changing with greater focus moving to outcomes.

'Now, with each new situation in this paradigm, there will only be creativity to come to the rescue. Being willing to look at new ways of doing things every time will now hold the key.'

Indraneel Roy Choudhury

'The new world will be highly driven by process, artificial intelligence, machine learning, robotics—the creativity to excel in these areas will be paramount. The general human mind will be tested more and more on digital platforms.'

Satyakam Basu

'In my opinion, for any successful enterprise, creativity and leadership are inseparable. Two of the most important jobs for any leader are to provide a vision for the enterprise, and to help remove barriers that stand in the way of achieving that vision.

Motivating people or organizations or causes or ideas takes creativity and leadership.

'How do leaders find new ways to keep their people engaged and positive? How do innovations in manufacturing occur? How do great sales managers build high-functioning teams with integrity? How do teachers create energetic and vibrant classrooms? All of these are functions requiring both leadership and a creative mind.

'Simply put, creativity combines with leadership when old answers to new challenges are exceeded by innovative thinking and determined execution. This will require further nurturing in the future world.'

Ashish Aul

'As we get away from social contact to a virtual and digital world, a paradigm shift is required in the way we connect with various stakeholders in the corporate world. We need to find new and innovative ways to reach out to teams, customers, vendors and peers.

'How we make an impact in a virtual environment is the new trait that every leader will have to learn. Every leader will have to think of creative ways of adding value, be it with regard to delivery models, cost optimization, enhancing revenues or retaining talent.'

Shyam Mamidi

'The digital and virtual world has thrown new challenges to leadership at all levels on how to engage more effectively, and creativity is the key to better engage with your peers and teams.

Leadership applies creativity to get right levels of participation, in motivating and praising team members. Leaders have also used creativity to figure out how to individually and collectively deal with issues in order to get the best outcome.

'Creativity as a leadership trait is now coming into every conversation and assignment, even monitoring and control activities, supported by digital technologies and analytics on hand. AI should take this creativity to the next level by carefully figuring out how engagement and discussions should differ for different individuals and teams based on situations and criticality of tasks.'

The new world will require us to remain flexible and adapt, which means leaders need to be agile all the time. Let us look at what that means for us.

8

Agile Leadership

Agood leader does not follow just one style of management; he or she modifies a style as required by a situation or culture. We often call this situational leadership, where one style never fits all, and the new-age leader needs to adopt whatever technique will deliver the best outcome.

Often, we confuse agile thinking with flexibility. They are different, and in this chapter, we are talking about leadership that is nimble-footed, or in other words, more alert. An agile style of management is about understanding the problem statement clearly and adapting to the needs as per data or tools available, instead of following a set pattern to arrive at a solution.

This is a requirement as in the future, teams will need even more flexibility, autonomy and power for decision-making as they become self-managed, operating mostly remotely.

Like any other style of leadership, agile leadership also needs a team to work together towards a common goal, and a leader needs to create an environment where there is collaboration among the teams, ensuring that they learn from each other and focus on continuous improvement. This also means empowering teams to take decisions.

One of the proven benefits of agile leadership is that response to stakeholders or customers is faster and decision-making is often quicker. Agile leadership thus cannot be successful if a leader tries to micro-manage, as the leader needs to let go so the team can arrive at a solution. This demands trust and ownership among team members, as they own the outcome. This style of leadership also helps an organization adapt to change faster than a more traditional approach. It also helps leaders grasp the needs of stakeholders and customers more closely, thus helping them get what they want.

An agile leader needs to ensure that a proper process is in place for the team to act, with a governance and pre-established review structure. He or she will intervene only when needed. This does not mean that the leader is absolved of all responsibility, as he or she is still accountable for the final delivery. And that's a difficult balance to strike since most traditional leaders are not comfortable with letting go and want to be hands-on while delivering an outcome. An agile leader ensures that the atmosphere is right for each member of the team to own the deliverables, take decisions and be successful, neither micro-managing nor leaving everything to others. And with the evolving world, the growing need for remote working and with the support of enabling technology, this new style of leadership is widely recognized as the need of the hour.

An agile leader believes that solutions evolve on a real-time basis and that the solutions of the past may not be the solutions of today as they need to change along with the times. Instead of relying on knowledge of the past, they depend more on cross-functional discussions to pool in more ideas and skills, so the teams who are self-managing might come up with solutions that have never been tried before. Moreover, these leaders want to be closer to their customers and stakeholders to understand the real issues and the solutions they are looking for, to focus on what is needed versus what can be offered. Customer centricity plays an important role.

A few months ago, my friend, who leads the global sales operations of a multinational based out of Germany, recruited Daniel to lead their European operations. He came from an oil and gas giant that is known for its agile culture and impressed the recruiter with his in-depth knowledge of the process.

Daniel joined the company in early 2020 and settled down well. In a short time, he was able to deliver results. And then the COVID-19 crisis hit the world and he was forced to operate from his home for the next few months. Projects that had been progressing well came almost to a standstill, and upon review, Daniel blamed the issues on the external crisis. He believed he was not able to drive the change that was needed as people were away from office and he had no direct control over them. Daniel presented his revised plan, and my friend accepted the delay in progress and agreed to the revised timelines.

But even after three months, nothing much had changed. A deep dive into the matter showed that Daniel had all the knowledge of agile ways of working, but it was only theoretical. In practice, he was a traditional manager who wanted direct control over his team members and did not adapt to the changing environment that had arisen due to COVID-19.

Where he failed was in empowering the team to take decisions, providing freedom and instilling a sense of trust. He did not stand by his people or establish clear responsibility and governance mechanisms, which are critical to lead in times of crisis.

When my friend spoke to Daniel about why he had not adapted to changing times, Daniel was clear in his thinking. He had been afraid that if he moved away from his own traditional style of management and granted too much autonomy to the team, then the power would be misused. Being new to the company, Daniel had also felt his leadership might be considered too friendly or weak by his team members. Daniel failed to ensure a balance between autonomy and control.

Following are a few important aspects of agile leadership that Daniel failed to practise.

Freedom and trust

An agile leader needs to understand the kind of freedom the team needs. The trend is clear: over time, most teams will be working remotely and won't be sitting next to each other. For agile working, the teams need not only a sense of freedom but also real freedom to act and take decisions as needed. And this means the leader needs to demonstrate trust. When the team takes a decision, it is possible that there will be some mistakes, and as an agile leader, he or she needs to own the mistakes made by the team members and stand by them as needed. This requires a change in mindset of the leader since it is easier said than done, but it is a critical component for promoting real ownership within the team.

Establishing clear deliverables

Ambiguity is never good in any form of leadership and agile leadership is no different. Deliverables need to be clear, with the teams and leader agreeing on timelines and what success will look like. Nothing should be left to guesswork, every expectation needs to be clear since the delivery will be driven and owned by the team members jointly.

Clear delegation

A leader needs to ensure that many aspects of decision-making are delegated to the team. The checks on the powers delegated need to be established to avoid ambiguity. Team members need to feel safe to act and take decisions, and ensuring that is a primary responsibility of an agile leader. A clear charter of individual responsibilities will help establish this. Any doubts need to be clarified to avoid delays in decision-making. The leader needs to define what the team can decide and what needs to flow upwards.

Culture of continuous improvement

Many organizations do claim to have a culture of continuous improvement, but in reality, this works more on paper than in practice. It takes a lot of commitment to create a truly agile way of working. An agile leader needs to ensure that the culture is actively promoted, the team is trained and can learn continuously while on the job. A culture in which curiosity and intelligent risk-taking are encouraged is important for success.

Provide continuous support

The agile way of working needs support from the top. Without the tools, systems and training, one should not expect results. A leader needs to understand the support required and ensure it is provided.

AGILE LEADERSHIP VOICES

Sarmila Basu

'While driving a mindset change in corporate culture and trying to bring his or her people along, the leader himself or herself needs to be highly adaptable to change. They need to practise "situational leadership" and not be rigid in their approach.'

Himal Tiwari

'The new paradigm will be dexterity across competencies, it will not be strategic versus operational, taskmaster versus democratic or the usual stereotypical one or the other binaries. The new leader will have to demonstrate competence across the scale.'

Nihil Dey

'Stay curious, stay agile and connect the dots. Be comfortable with "failing fast" and reinventing basis learnings.'

Diptendu Mondal

'In today's world, obsolescence of technology along with a very short product life-cycle period has become the norm. In keeping with this fast rate of change, we each have to be alert, proactive and agile in taking action. We will not be able to enjoy the laurels of past success for long. Instead, we need to be on our toes, update and align ourselves with the fast-changing ecosystem. Those who do not accept that change is the only constant will perish without any notice.

'For instance, the ecosystem of the automobile industry is changing fast. If electric vehicles come to market at a reasonable cost, there will be a huge impact on the automobile service industry, and leaders will have to adapt to this new reality.'

Sandeep Batra

'Be agile, especially from a technology point of view. Technology is not the domain of the chief information officer anymore. Seize the moment and become the tech evangelist for your organization. You may be the only one to survive!'

Haresh Hemrajani

'The key principles of agile methodologies will remain the same in the post-COVID-19 world. However, the interaction will transform into a hybrid approach where teams/sprints members will be distributed over multiple locations. The need is for digital tools/applications to capture daily stand-up meetings, digital boards/portals to highlight task allocation and to visually facilitate tracking of team progress.

'In the post-COVID-19 world, independent portions of tasks derived from a composite project will have to be tackled by a disparate workforce in a distributed location. Essentially, agile principles have been fast-tracked by COVID-19. Corporates will need to reorganize from hierarchical to more agile organization structures as well as introduce self-management practices, track employee burnout and re-train leaders to manage in the new world.'

The virtual world pulls us apart and technology connects us once again. The opportunity to stay in touch with people far away and thus expand our networks has never been as easy as it is today. Why not capitalize on such possibilities?

9

Digital Networking

Experts say many issues can be solved not by how much you know, but who you know. Times have proven that meaningful networking can be highly beneficial for personal and professional growth. With the technology now in place, the number of people we can stay in touch with is exponentially higher than ever before.

Over time, the world became bigger and bigger as we spread across geographies.

Today, we live in a century where we might stay miles apart, but thanks to technology, we are able to connect seamlessly, can be in touch with our near and dear ones every moment, maintain relationships with multiple people even without meeting them, even when we are not next to each other. Lost connections are easy to rebuild. Physical boundaries and distance don't affect us anymore. Information is available freely, helping us to enrich our interactions.

Thus, not being connected with others is an unacceptable option; we, hence, need to master the art of staying in touch.

When I joined the corporate world, my first boss advised me to get to know people beyond my horizon, to network intelligently. The more you network, the more you increase your ability to build your net worth—be it in terms of success or knowledge, he said.

Wise advice, I must say. I never even dreamt of a day when you might be recruited for a top job in Europe while living in Asia by a professional search consultant based in Africa. That is the power of digital networking in a world where global has become local.

Digital networking facilitates breaking boundaries. It helps build a much wider network, opens our minds to different viewpoints, and breeds diversity through interaction with people from different cultures, backgrounds and economic status, which is important to build a balanced outlook. I also find digital networking to be a great way to learn in today's world. We can now choose to follow many people who used to be difficult to reach and interact with by simply connecting on different digital platforms, through websites and blogs or by attending webinars.

Networking has both pros and cons. If not managed well, it can take a toll on you as it requires you to invest time and energy, and both these resources are limited. These days, we often hear about people who are addicted to social media, how they start believing in fake news and get influenced by it. I differentiate between social media and digital networking. While usage of social media is much more generic in nature, digital networking is quite focused, with a purpose in mind.

There is a lot to be learnt from the story of Shankar, a past colleague of mine, who now lives in Chicago. Shankar currently heads the North American sales of a large dairy manufacturer. I have seen Shankar grow professionally over the past many years and one thing that has always struck me has been the way he keeps in touch with the people he knows. While living in Amsterdam, whenever I meet someone travelling here from India, to my surprise, I find most of them know Shankar. It seems like all 1.3 billon people on the subcontinent have had a brush with Shankar—he makes the world look so small. And then he stays in touch with a fair number of them. I even know of people whom he has interviewed just once, who have not even been selected for the job in question, but are still in touch with him. I have always been curious why and how Shankar keeps so many connections alive, and I finally reached out to him to find out more.

Shankar was happy to explain his approach to networking. He said that for him, any meeting is the start of a relationship. He likes to explore the connection. It is not that he keeps the connection with an ulterior motive in mind, however, he is curious about where that relationship might lead and what he could give back that would make him, or the other person, a better individual.

Shankar is clear about why he wants to network. He has a 'network grid' and once he figures out how a person fits into it, he invests time in developing his relationship with the person. This could be through simple text messages, or phone calls, or by following someone on LinkedIn, Instagram or Facebook. His network grid includes the media he wants to use for a person, the frequency of interaction and the purpose, which helps him with time management. And every year, he refreshes the list, dropping some names and adding others.

'Life is much easier now that people don't expect to know you face-to-face, as digital networking is accepted,' says Shankar

Shankar's methods of digital networking may be too exacting to be feasible for all, but defining a clear strategy and ways of interaction will certainly help many of us remain connected in the digital world.

In the past sections, I said that leaders who are well networked will have an advantage in the future. Indeed, digital networking is a huge opportunity if done with care and attention. Following are a few points to take away from Shankar's story.

Decide why you need to network

Asking yourself why you need to network will make your goal clear. While networking can be quite generic in nature, it can also be focused. For example, if you are looking to change your job, you should network among people who can help you professionally or personally with your goal. However, if you wish to, say, publish a book that reaches many people, your networking needs will be very different. Hence, the first step is to decide the goal, both short term and long term, which will then lead you to the next steps of figuring out who you should approach and when. It is expected that you will refresh your goals on a periodic basis, but without a goal of some sort, digital networking efforts may be meaningless.

Profile your network

In today's data-driven world, digital networking needs to be data driven as well. Once your goal is clear, you can profile your network and draw up a list of possibilities. Since time is limited and we are all busy with our own lives, a profiling exercise can help eliminate those with whom you do not need to network. This will help you draw up a shortlist of names so you can focus on the people who matter, and you should be clear on why they matter. To make the right selections, explore information already available on social networks. This will help you match your requirements and interest levels to avoid wasting time and energy.

Choose the right mediums

There are many platforms these days to help you network easily. While we have simple, proven tools like calling or emailing, you can explore other social media channels or mediums. You need to also understand the tone and method of communicating on the different platforms in order to deliver your message clearly. Then you can decide what suits you. There is nothing to suggest that LinkedIn will work better than keeping in touch with an old associate through a simple WhatsApp message. My only advice is that you should choose wisely as you can't be everywhere and spend all your time on networking.

You should choose a mix of mediums as needed at various points in time, however, one needs to be careful about how, when and for what you are using each one. Learning which tool delivers to what kind of audience will be of immense help. For example, Facebook may not be the right place to look for a job change, just like LinkedIn may not be the forum to publish a photo of a beautiful sunset captured during a holiday to let people know how relaxed you were after a hard month of work. But there are always exceptions to a rule.

Allocate time

We are all hard-pressed for time. There are just twenty-four hours in a day, after all. Digital networking can eat up many hours unless managed properly. I have seen people getting exhausted and even burning out just to keep pace with networking. My advice would be to allocate time, add it to your calendar and make it part of your daily routine. This way you will know when to act and how much time to spend, or else you may get carried away.

So, define your own strategy, as only you know best what you want and what suits you.

Balance

While we have spoken about the opportunities that digital networking offers in today's world, we need to keep in mind that 'virtual coffee' will not replace all face-to-face meetings. Traditional networking will not go away and will always be a preferred option for many people. Striking a balance between traditional and digital networking will always be best.

DIGITAL NETWORKING VOICES

Nihil Dey

'All things digital have forced a level of unprecedented change on our industry. But at another more fundamental level, it has also resulted in reinforcing the need to build strong, meaningful real-world relationships more than ever before.

'In a world where we have five hundred Facebook friends but less than five who will make the effort to meet you in person to wish you for your birthday, it's evident that real, person-to-person contact is being replaced by the more convenient virtual interface. Translate this into the professional domain of public relations, which has as its building blocks one simple fundamental—the ability to influence the influencers. If you don't have a strong meaningful relationship with the influencers of tomorrow, you will not be able to deliver the outcomes clients want.

'So, I believe that at two different ends of the spectrum we will see change: the professionals of tomorrow will need to embrace new technology on the one hand, but on the other, they will also need to embrace genuine human connections. Those who learn how to play at both ends of the spectrum will effortlessly straddle the intersection of the real and virtual worlds and become the leaders of tomorrow.'

Subroto Gupta

'It is statistically improbable that the smartest people in any given field already work for you. Leadership in the future will be all about nurturing and building an external network of advisors, solution providers and opportunity creators who can help in ensuring that the organization reads the environment better and responds faster and more effectively to change.'

Vineet Kapila

'Leadership has two dimensions: behaviour and values. In terms of values, I don't think anything will change, we will still need to be ethical, empathic, supportive, spiritual, and community-sensitive. Whereas on the behaviour side, they will need to change. It is okay for leaders not to have all the answers. But they need to know where they can find the answers. The leaders will have to leverage wider stakeholder network to deliver results; they will need a wider connect to have the worldview to achieve results.'

Himal Tiwari

'The new leader will be an engaging one who demonstrates the capability to be ambidextrous and stay connected to people within and outside the organization. Leading laterally across informal and formal organization networks will be a key priority for the new-gen leader.'

Haresh Hemrajani

'COVID-19 has introduced one important change, which is the ability to be contacted via a video call service. While these services have been prevalent for some time, it is now a generally accepted protocol to seek meetings with internal and/or external and/or unknown contacts and expect video conference calls. The world has transformed with business users today switching between disparate video calls (Teams, Zoom, Meet) throughout the working day.'

The virtual world will give rise to emotions and, as leaders, we need to handle them with care. While we all need to be emotionally resilient, we also need to ensure every individual feels safe in the virtual world: embraced, appreciated and accepted as they are. Let us look at how we can create a safe environment for our workforce.

10

Psychological Safety

It may sound judgmental, but many people do believe that the traditional corporate environment is a rat race to beat co-workers to the top. Some even believe that it's dangerous to be yourself and one needs to mimic certain behaviours and display certain traits to survive there.

I won't go there, but what I find is in our changing world, the future will be a lot about leading a team that thrives in a safe, inclusive environment and can discuss and contribute openly without the fear of being shot down.

There have been studies about this topic, and it has been observed that a team whose members feel psychologically safe around each other often becomes a high-performing team. In the new, fast-changing, technologically driven world, innovations are at the centre of any business, and we need everyone to contribute and lead, not only be led. And such a culture can be promoted only If the team feels valued and psychologically safe

One of the important aspects of psychological safety is that it is not about the individual winning or losing, it is about winning as a team that matters in the end. It takes continuous effort for a leader to instil this clarity in a team. A leader needs to create an atmosphere where every member participates without judgement, or fear of being judged, is willing to take risks even at the cost of failure, to voice their opinions openly and not feel insecure at any point of time. This also means that every member of the team needs to be honest with each other and should have the ability to admit their mistakes.

I often wonder how we can measure psychological safety. I am not sure if we can or should convert it into metrics. If the kind of feeling and atmosphere we are aiming for truly exists, the success of the team will tell us we have achieved our goal, so I wouldn't be too concerned about how to formally measure it.

Through 2020 and 2021, I have been observing different teams' effectiveness as they have started working remotely due to the COVID-19 situation. One of my favourite leaders is Shirley Johnson, whom I have known for many years. Shirley leads a large team based in London. We were colleagues years ago, and we still talk often and share our thoughts with each other.

During one of our evening chats, I asked Shirley how she was dealing with the situation, with people feeling much more vulnerable due to the pandemic, being locked down and working from home. I was sure the teams must miss the face-to-face interactions with and support of their leaders.

Instead of answering, Shirley asked me a question instead. 'Where do you feel the safest?'

'At home,' I replied.

'That would be my answer too. Why do you think you are safest at home?'

'I trust my family members, I can be myself, I can share my thoughts without being judged, and my family is willing to support me if I am going through a bad patch.'

'We all spend more time at work than in our homes, is it not?' asked Shirley. 'So why should our work life be any different? Shouldn't we feel equally safe at our workplace?'

Shirley said that for her team, nothing had changed due to the pandemic, that it was business as usual. A team that is well-knit stays together, she said, with every member fully trusting the others with a minimum of politics. She had set a few boundaries and agreed on values—such as no one is allowed to talk behind anyone's back, every idea needs to be listened to, opinions are to be respected and debated before decisions are taken—and she had ensured that the team followed them.

In the past two years, the attrition in Shirley's team has been less than 5 per cent, and she believes that this has been possible only because every member feels safe and valued. Shirley said that everyone in the team behaves as though they are an entrepreneur, coming out with new ideas, sharing thoughts openly even though they might be deemed 'stupid'. As a leader, Shirley says her main job is to ensure the team has a shared vision and values, operates within the rules of the organization and has established boundaries, and that is what drives her success as a leader.

There are a few important lessons the new-age leader can learn from Shirley to promote a psychologically safe team.

Agree on team values

To build a safe environment, as a leader, you need to agree on the values the team will stand on and remind the team of these periodically. So, first spend time defining these values, which will later help to call out inappropriate behaviours that could damage the psychological safety of the team.

Be yourself

As a leader, you need to create the confidence that each team member can be themselves within the team, that no one needs to pretend, and that they will be accepted as they are. This means they can be free to share ideas and challenge each other's thoughts without being afraid of being judged.

Conflict is okay

In the corporate world, conflict is often seen as negative; however, I see conflict in a different light. If the conflict is not due to a personal win or loss or to satisfy one's ego, it can be healthy. The team needs to be mature enough to deal with positive conflict in a manner that will enhance the performance of the team.

Be creative

Any idea is welcome, no matter how irrelevant it may sound at first. Each idea will be evaluated as needed and, as a leader, you need to ensure each member of the team knows that their contribution is respected and valued. You need to encourage exploration of new ideas keeping the end goal in mind.

Stand by each other

A team that thrives on psychological safety will value each other and stand by each other. Together they will complete the puzzle. No one is perfect and no one has all the qualities that are required for a team to succeed. It is the leader's job to ensure that this value is promoted within the team. You need to demonstrate that it is okay to make mistakes, and no one will be punished. In fact, there is nothing wrong with admitting your mistakes in front of others as no one is superhuman. This simple ideology gives the team huge psychological safety.

Remain curious

A curious mind always breeds new ideas, and as a leader, one needs to ensure the team is a safe space to explore new avenues. Without curiosity, innovative ideas won't surface. You need to remain curious and ask questions instead of directing. That will demonstrate that you also need to constantly learn and will give the team the confidence to ask relevant questions.

Trust

No team can excel if there is no trust among its members. A leader needs to demonstrate trust towards each member of the team equally to ensure openness at every stage. He or she needs to promote a culture in which each member trusts the others in the team as well, and that can only happen if everyone feels equally safe.

Feedback

This is an important tool for anyone, and when a leader ensures that the team is psychologically safe, feedback can flow. A leader needs to ensure that feedback is handled with respect and is taken into consideration as work progresses. Feedback should be given on time and adequately.

PSYCHOLOGICAL SAFETY VOICES

Diptendu Mondal

'Work-from-home brings a lack of face-to-face interaction among employees, and reduced departmental and cross-functional face-to-face interactions. It is a big change in terms of the way people used to develop bonding and chemistry among individuals and teams. We need a culture where we have constant engagement among individuals and teams, not only to perform our responsibilities but also to keep the personal touch, maintain a sense of belonging and mentoring. Leaders carry a very important role in executing a smooth transition from traditional ways of working to doing jobs through virtual presence. They need to find ways for team members to celebrate their successes together and share the joys and sorrows of their day-to-day journeys. In fact, leaders have to develop a framework that can percolate this way of working across the organization in order to avoid the feeling of psychological detachment.'

Naveen Begwani

'Take tough decisions yet remain compassionate. In these changing times, while balancing the top line and bottom line, showing resilience is quite important. A leader may have to take some difficult decisions, which may be necessary for the larger good of the business and associates. Some of these choices, especially when it pertains to employees, need to be executed in a respectful and gracious manner. Make them feel safe.'

Suman Ghose

'In our training sessions on emotional intelligence, I often get asked this question: Can I show empathy to my team, won't it make me look weak? My short answer is always this: Listening, showing compassion and empathy mean that you try to understand them, but does not mean you have to agree with them. As Stephen Covey puts it nicely in his book *The Seven Habits of Highly Effective People*, we need to listen to understand, not just listen to respond.

'The famous author John Steinbeck wrote almost a century ago: "In every bit of honest writing in the world ... there is a base theme. Try to understand men, if you understand each other, you will be kind to each other. Knowing a man well never leads to hate and nearly always leads to love." Empathy and compassion are powerful traits and are required more than ever in this new world order, and lead to psychological safety.'

Anil Nashier

'Making mistakes and being able to talk about them must be at the heart of developing a disruptive business model. Understanding and mastering psychological safety becomes the critical ingredient towards building a dream team for this purpose. Building a culture of team over individual talent is a great way of developing a psychological safety net. It is crucial for leadership to demonstrate empathy and nurture a collaborative environment through leading by example.'

Sameer Agarwal

'As a leader, it is critical to make your team physically and psychologically safe to help build trust and loyalty. This motivates them, driving significantly higher performance. We need to have empathy and listen to our teams effectively, which will show that the leader is engaged and understands and supports them. Teams need to be empowered and made a part of the decision-making process, which will provide visibility to their accomplishments. Last but not least, the team feels psychologically safe if they know what is required of them and they have the freedom and support to achieve it, sometimes even by making mistakes.'

Communication is probably the most important tool for leadership, and all of us are continuously learning to communicate better. Do we need to relook at how we communicate in the virtual world?

11

Communication

Over the last few years, the physical distance between us may have increased, but most of us would agree that we still feel connected. We may not be under the same roof breathing the same air, but we can communicate easily, see each other over video calls and work together, even though we are apart, to deliver a common goal. News about events happening in other parts of the world reaches us in no time; we no longer have to wait for the morning newspaper to be updated.

Communication is all about exchanging information and thoughts, and the digital world has opened up so many modes of communication. Today, we are no longer limited to face-to-face interactions, exchange of physical letters, emails, messages or even phone calls. In fact, there are so many ways of communicating nowadays that making the right, efficient choice can be overwhelming.

In the virtual world, communication takes place when people are not at the same location. Thus, it is important to be clear in what we want to say in order to remove any ambiguity. This clarity will encourage collaboration and alignment in decision-making, moving everyone towards a common objective. Many unspoken words need to be spoken in a way that the other person, in spite of being physically distant, is clear about what we want to actually say, or else, chances of misunderstanding arise.

Let me tell you the story of Priyanka, an Indian executive who moved to Amsterdam about seven years ago. Priyanka was a successful leader who had worked across multinational corporations, and her last job had been heading the supply chain in Asia for her organization.

Priyanka had done her initial years of schooling in London, and then her family had moved to India when she was fourteen years old, and she had completed her higher education there. Her job allowed her to travel widely across the globe due to her involvement in international projects. She had always had an interest in people, and working across multiple cultures and cross-functional teams had helped her develop invaluable people skills. Priyanka was regarded as an asset to the company and as her next step, she was offered a role in company headquarters in Amsterdam to lead a critical project.

Priyanka was known to be courageous and to call a spade a spade. She never shied away from critical conversations. Furthermore, she was aware of the differences in the ways of working between India and the Western world. She knew her new role would call for a new way of working. So, before moving to Amsterdam, she took stock of the adjustments she thought she would need to make to her management style in order to be successful in her new world.

Priyanka's first project in the new location was to automate supply chain activities in the Netherlands. Her organization had only one office in the country, which was a benefit to Priyanka as her team and stakeholders were all in the same location. She managed to deliver on all milestones of the project, and in no time, she emerged as a star performer, and the global supply chain head was given a lot of kudos for bringing her to the role.

In about two years, the project was complete, and due to her terrific performance, Priyanka was promoted to head the global projects team, in which capacity all country project teams would report to her. Now Priyanka's wings indeed spread across the globe. But for Priyanka, this marked a sudden shift. She was not used to leading her team virtually, barely getting a chance to meet anyone face-to-face. She was out of her comfort zone.

Over time, she realized that many things had changed, and that something was missing in her leadership style. With projects not progressing as she would like, she started feeling the pressure. In a few months, more feedback came in and the situation was brought to the attention of the executive committee, with Priyanka being labelled a non-performer.

The global head of supply chain was not amused. How could a person performing so well for years fail in a new role? He went deep into the case and realized it had nothing to do with Priyanka's intention or knowledge; the stumbling block was her challenges with virtual leadership and the way she was communicating with her team. The common thread in all complaints about her was that the team was not able to understand her, and that she did not trust her team.

Priyanka was offered help. Then more issues were identified: she was directional in her approach, she made decisions before discussing, she was only bothered about the task and did not care about the team, her attention span for listening was poor, she did not encourage new ideas, she was not clear about her objectives.

The team also felt she was not updated on the latest tools and technologies, still relying on old formats for communication such as the telephone or email. In summary, Priyanka needed to learn the virtual ways of communicating effectively since all her life she had dealt with teams who were located in the same physical space as her.

The feedback was shared with Priyanka and today, after four years, Priyanka has taken over as the global supply chain head for the company when her boss retired. She adapted.

Here's what we can take away from Priyanka's story:

Be present

This is probably the most important but most difficult to execute. In the digital world, you are not physically present next to the person or the team you are talking to, which is all the more reason to ensure that everyone feels you are present mentally. We are all hard-pressed for time, and it would be only natural to juggle a few balls by multitasking while you are on calls. But once your audience knows your attention is not on them, you will lose them.

Listening attentively is becoming ever more important, which is possible only if you are present mentally and making an effort to understand and ask relevant questions. Remember, you do not have the benefit of walking down the corridor to see your colleague to resolve any misunderstandings, so make these calls count.

Know your audience

Knowledge about whom we are speaking to always helps. This old rule is even more relevant in today's digital world since being remote complicates delivery of our message in many ways unless we are absolutely clear.

Ensure two-way dialogue

To communicate effectively, dialogue is always preferred to a monologue. Ensure two-way communication, even when not present in person. A great tool, after listening carefully, is to acknowledge and validate what you have understood, followed by logical questions. This facilitates participation and helps you remain curious about what the other person or team has to say. Your curiosity will encourage others to discuss new ideas and promote a culture of inclusion that is a must for innovation. Feedback after dialogue is also a great tool to ensure that your message has landed effectively, be it with your own team or with external parties, since nothing is worse than others missing the point of your communication.

Know the red and green buttons

Virtual communication calls for more awareness of what may trigger a stress response in your audience, otherwise known as activating the 'red buttons'. Since many a time communication happens over a medium that is not face-to-face, being aware of sensitivities helps tailor your conversation and avoid uncomfortable situations. You should also be aware of 'green buttons', or those topics that can make your audience feel comfortable and open. This awareness can only come if you know the people you are interacting with well enough or spend some time studying them. It is not a waste of effort.

Avoid data overload

Today, most information is available at our fingertips; there is a lot more data available than ever before. As leaders, be mindful of selecting and bringing in the right data and avoid junk overload that can lead to what we call 'analysis paralysis'. You need to understand what is needed, and how much is needed.

Choose platforms carefully

The digital world gives us many more options than we had before. To be effective in your communication, you need to carefully choose the medium to reach your target audience. There are experts in these areas: engage with them, appoint them if necessary. Even if you are not in a marketing or sales function where you deal with external customers, I believe every manager needs a communication strategy. Why not take help from specialists?

Remain updated

You need to remain updated almost on a real-time basis about new technology, as it is evolving even as we speak. Look at options that are user-friendly, cost-effective and secure to reach your target audience faster and more effectively. You can always invest in new technology if you know what is available and what works for you, so spend time getting to know the alternatives and the value they can bring to you.

COMMUNICATION VOICES

Pranesh Chatterjee

'Leaders currently functional in different positions within an organization are probably not prepared to accept the ways the work environment is going to change in the future. The changes will be multiple, with several consequences. The work life of an employee is likely to become more dynamic in nature. Leaders have to think about reasonably acceptable solutions to keep skilled people in the workforce because they tend to leave the company at the slightest provocation. They have to improve and, if required, alter their communication skills and styles to a very high level and keep their eyes wide open. This, along with the openness of mind, will govern whether the manager will be able to carry forward a group of highly skilled workers. In the future work environment, transparency in management will be necessary because several modes of cross-checking will be available in the advanced digital world. This means the leaders of the current generation will have to learn to speak out more openly—which in turn demands a big change in the mindset of managers.'

Naveen Begwani

'Communicate, communicate, communicate. Nothing can replace the power of communication. While the medium of communication would undergo a change, the messaging needs to be designed in a manner that not only allays any fears that the associates may have, but also continuously reassures them. Keep the team engaged and don't let the organization lose sight of the larger objective.'

Deepa Dey

'In our well-wired world, for the most meaningful, sustainable connection, we need to disconnect to connect. The white noise generated by the deluge of information is overwhelming. Astute professionals will disconnect from this to focus on real experience to create benchmarks of truth. And this will be clutter-breaking. This means we need to relearn how we communicate in the new world.'

Shridhar Narayan

'Effective communication is not just about talking. It is also about active listening. In a digital world driven by communication and a desire to connect, it is easy to get lost in a fog of information and take the act of listening for granted.

'Listening is the foundation of communication and the key to building strong relationships. Listening to your team members and understanding their problems and concerns in delivering their objectives forms a key trait of any successful leader.'

Sameer Agarwal

'Communication has dramatically changed from speech to postal services to electronic media to the various chat and social platforms that have led the way in virtual communication. The way humans interact has been permanently altered. As we continue to make strides here, humans must learn, unlearn and relearn on a continuous basis to ensure that they don't turn into robots and are able to effectively communicate with empathy.'

The new-age workforce needs independence. They are much more informed and capable of making decisions. The virtual world also calls for agility, and hence empowerment will be a key element for future leaders. Let us see why it is a leadership trait we must adopt.

12

Brand Yourself

A personal brand is all about *you*—your values, your passion, the way you would like to be known or perceived by others. It is about your uniqueness, what differentiates you from others. It is similar to any corporate branding exercise, but here the brand is you.

Over time, your 'brand' will establish who you are and what you stand for, and through this effort, you will be highlighting your strengths and your areas of interest. You will be identified with a set of values and competencies that will give you your unique identity. This will differentiate you from the rest.

There are many books and articles on personal branding. I am also aware of the extensive templates that have been developed that can help and guide you. I strongly recommend getting external help to get you started.

Here are five quick tips on building your personal brand:

Determine what you would like to be known for

You should know what *you* want to be known for, and this is something that is completely up to you to decide. For example, among your colleagues, someone might want to be known as a technological wizard, while another might want their executional capabilities to be their top draw. It is up to you to determine, but it is important that you start working on it. To do that, you need to understand yourself. You need to know your strengths, your competencies and your likes. Start reflecting on who you are, and over time, you will discover your niche.

If I may share a bit of my personal story, I am by education a finance professional, but I wanted to go beyond finance and explore new learnings. Over time, I realized my biggest interest was in 'people' and I found leadership traits to be a fascinating subject. I started observing people around me—how they acted, how they reacted, what made them stand out, what made them successful, what made them smile, what made them fail at times, how they reacted on a good day, why a particular event triggered a reaction only in some people and so on. It's a long list.

This clarity helped me be consistent in my journey to be an author, observing daily moments, sharing corporate stories and learnings. Unfortunately, I did not realize the importance of personal branding at the right time. All my posts and events should have been directed to the cause/purpose I believed in, which is constantly upskilling ourselves, and I should have shared more corporate stories to ensure that the theme of continuous learning is embraced by others. My learning, hence, is that once you figure out your mission, do not procrastinate—start sharing your voice as soon as you can. Life lost is opportunity lost.

Identify the purpose you stand for

The world is changing, and many professionals care much more about purpose than just earning money. If you can figure out the purpose you stand or live for—that is, what you are passionate about—you can channel your energy in that direction while building your brand. A deep look at yourself may be the first step towards finding your purpose, unless you are already aware of it.

Be clear about who you want to reach

Once you know what you want to achieve, define who all you want to reach. If you are in the corporate world and want to build your brand for the next role or job, your audience will be very different from, for example, if you were a freelancer and wanted to build computer games or design web pages. Knowing who you want to reach will help you determine the channels you would like to use; the next point is about that.

Determine how you want to get there

Now that you know what you want and who you want to reach, it is time to work on the stories you want to tell and choose the channels you would like to use to share your stories. For example, many recruiters use LinkedIn for recruitment and if your goal is to look for the next opportunity, you might choose to be visible there. Or you may choose to focus on your current role, and as many organizations have their own internal social media forums, you may choose to share your thoughts and express your opinions there. There can be other channels too. It all depends on what you want to share, and then the 'how' follows.

Explore the new you and adjust the brand requirement

What interests you today might change over time. The more you work on your personal brand, the more awareness you will gain about yourself. So, keep exploring who you are. Your brand image can be altered over time, though it takes effort.

By building your brand, you can create a differentiator for yourself, which will help you in your career or in your daily life. The best part is you will discover what you stand for, what your purpose is.

You are a brand by yourself even if you do not realize it, so it is important that you take control of it and decide for yourself what you stand for—your own brand versus being led by others' perceptions of you.

However, be consistent with your approach and have a clear plan. Start-stop-start may not be the best approach. I have seen many professionals getting too excited about building their brand, and that actually hampers their progress and learning. My suggestion is start slow and chew on it. You have enough time.

As Jeff Bezos says, 'Your brand is what other people say about you when you are not in the room.'

BRAND YOURSELF VOICES

Anil Nashier

'Personal branding is taking control of your own digital footprint during today's war of talent. It's crucial to take control of your own brand rather than being one assembled by algorithms of search engines. Trust and authenticity, as exhibited by strong brands, always allow deeper connection with individuals.

Establishing and leveraging your network by clearly articulating your own positioning and value system towards your target audiences is a vital part of brand building.'

Satyakam Basu

'Personal branding helps to build a direct bridge between you and others based on your authenticity and credibility. It increases aspirations of others to be within your network, and helps build you a robust personal network. Hence, it helps you gain more confidence to stand on your own reputation rather than piggybacking off other persons/companies/platforms. A must-do in the new world.'

Arunabha Ghosh

'By building your brand, you can create a differentiator for yourself—you know what you stand for and what your purpose is. I have seen many people start but then leave it undone. One must be consistent in his/her approach and must have a clear plan; start-stop-start won't work.'

Puneet Gupta

'In my view, minimum 80 per cent of the professionals are mostly "followers" and the rest end up being "leaders". The differentiator between the two, other than the intellectual quotient and conceptual clarity, is their perception among others. Are they seen as someone who can be followed? Someone who can be trusted? Someone who can foresee better? Someone who has strong ethics? Personal branding always helps create that perception.'

13

Empowerment

Will empowerment in the new world be different from the traditional empowerment skills we want our leaders to have?

I look at empowerment simply: to me, it means delegating tasks and allowing employees to control their actions, taking decisions within a framework to achieve an objective without being supervised at every moment. This means added responsibility and authority levels for team members—responsibility that was previously with the leader. More autonomy and decision-making in the hands of teams makes them less dependent than in traditional hierarchical ways of working, in which many decisions need the approval of a higher authority.

Empowerment is thus about creating a culture that enables employees to act, allowing them to control things without asking for permission at every stage.

It is, however, hard to let go. So many leaders end up paying lip service to empowerment, still wanting to control everything in an unstated way. In practice, this amounts to telling people to take decisions but then also telling them to take approval before acting. That does not work.

We have read about how the world is moving from control to inclusion; as new-age leaders, we know how the contributions of each member of a team are important. Empowerment is hence about giving and about creating a culture around it. This is possible only through intentional action from leaders to support teams with the right tools and information. The manager's role is to ensure that they provide support and create a conducive environment for teams to thrive.

My friend Lluis told me a story about how he solved recruitment issues in one of the country offices he was responsible for. I find it fascinating how simple steps to empower teams can change a culture and solve long-standing problems.

A few years ago, when Lluis was the business head of a large MNC's European operations, the company came under pressure to control costs as revenues were not growing in line with expectations. So the top management decided on a hiring freeze, and any recruitment needed to be approved by the global chief operating officer, whom Lluis reported to.

Lluis followed the process. He had reasonable attrition in his department, but he managed to get the required approvals on time from the chief operating officer. However, the resources management team was not able to fill the positions in a timely manner, which led to poor or no handover between the employee who was leaving and the new recruit, leading to huge frustration in the region.

The reason for the delay, said talent resourcing, was the non-availability of the right resources in the market due to high demand in that area. This was surprising since the MNC had one of the best-known brands in the region. Lluis knew that people took pride in working for his organization.

The longest delays in filling positions was in Portugal. Lluis examined the entire process, from requisition to hiring, and realized it took eleven approvals before a candidate was offered a job. And of these eleven steps, eight required approvals from headquarters. When Lluis asked the head of HR whether he was aware of the situation, the answer was negative. It became clear to Lluis that though he had an efficient recruiting team, they were bogged down by bureaucracy due to the over-engineered approval process.

Lluis proposed a few changes. First, he standardized the roles instead of treating each role as unique. This itself brought down the type of roles by 70 per cent with standard job descriptions. Secondly, he clearly defined what was expected from each role, the experience level and skills required and the salary ranges. And lastly, he took advantage of the digital world, installing a new system to automate the end-to-end process. And most importantly, he pushed the decision-making to the countries by limiting the approval process to three steps, out of which only one involved headquarters.

It was a big change. As the pilot took off in Portugal, it was a success and was rolled out to the regional level. It took a few months, but finally the resource issue was solved. The next year, the same recruitment team that was blamed for inefficiency won the global best team award from the CEO of the company.

Let us summarize the learnings from Lluis's story.

Create an open environment

Empowerment is a two-way process. While, as a leader, you delegate authority and decision-making to your team, at the same time you want to make them feel elevated in their roles in order for them to take ownership over decisions and deliver. It is important to create an open environment where discussions are encouraged and new ideas are valued. This openness creates the feeling that each team member is wanted and valued—an essential ingredient for an empowered team.

Be clear about boundaries

Define the authority and responsibility matrix. A clear RACI (responsibility, authority, consulted, informed) chart is always helpful for defining what is expected from whom. Back that up with a schedule which will define authority for each role, along with the dos and don'ts. This will help employees know what they can decide and what they can't, and will remove ambiguity as everyone will be on the same page.

Remain accountable

Empowering your team does not mean that you, as a leader, are absolved of all accountability; you still have a job to do, which is ensuring that the tasks are delivered on time, at the right quality and agreed cost. One of the important tasks of the leader is to ensure that his or her team knows that the leader is there to own responsibility and is accountable for the outcome.

Create clear processes and governance

Clear governance and defined processes are key to empowerment. Every review meeting needs to be clearly defined. Invest effort in creating clear standard processes and encourage teams to follow them. One of the biggest risks in empowered teams arises when they begin to develop their own processes, which should be discouraged.

Anticipate and manage risk

The digital world is not free from risk; we all know about the increase in cybercrimes with every passing day. As a leader, put adequate controls and measures in place to secure the environment against these crimes so that the team can work with less worries in mind. There will always be a chance of mistakes being made by empowered teams, and as a leader, you need to be clear that you are okay with this and are willing to accept that risk—but only as long as those mistakes were made with the proper intentions.

Build trust

Trust always flows two ways: you can delegate your tasks by trusting your team, similarly, your employees also need to trust you. If you lose your team's trust, empowerment will fail. You need to stand by them if they commit a mistake or take a wrong decision, and use the lessons from such failures for their development and to secure the future.

Ensure continuous training and development

Build your team's confidence by developing them continuously. Every day new technologies are hitting the market. Encourage your team to grow their expertise so that they also possess the skills you have as a leader. This will give the team the confidence to step into your shoes and take informed decisions. The investment in your team will be paid back in no time.

Recognize efforts

Appreciation works, especially when done with genuine intent. Ensure that you and your senior leaders appreciate the efforts of the empowered teams. Recognize them; broadcast their achievements to other teams. This will in turn encourage everyone else to step up and embrace the culture that is required for empowered organizations.

EMPOWERMENT VOICES

Himal Tiwari

'Developing an enabling culture will be a key priority for all leaders. The theme will be developing a culture and not a cult. The leaders will allow space for employees to find their own connection with the organization and their own meaning and value in doing so.'

Surajit Banerjee

'The days of close supervision are gone. In a world where we are socially and physically distanced, every professional will need both physical and mental space to manage their turf and that is what the work-scape of tomorrow will be.'

Naveen Begwani

'Delegate, empower and trust. Groom the team to take decisions, allow them to take risk. Have the ability and the courage to fail. Fail fast, gather the learnings and move on. Be agile, encourage and empower your team to try new technologies, to add new skills. That is the way to develop more leaders. If one is a finance associate, how can the leader help transform oneself to a data scientist? If one is an HR resource, how can the leader assist oneself in creating and retaining a talent pool which is fit for purpose. Challenging times are the best times to get the best talent! And you will get the best talent if you can create a culture that empowers.'

Anushree Singh

'If the need of the hour is to respond with speed, innovation and creativity, then we will have to allow decision-making closer to market. New ways of working can only be successful with trust and empowerment. With empowerment comes responsibility and growth. To engage and drive new-age professionals, we will have to provide space to work, take decisions and freedom to exercise judgment.'

Shyam Mamidi

'COVID-19 tested the preparedness and resiliency of not only corporates but also individuals, families, small and medium businesses, entrepreneurs, government agencies. Very clearly, not everyone was prepared for this long overhaul and neither had a clear business continuity plan or contingency to the extent needed.

'This was a testing time for the corporates. The magnitude of impact in some industries was massive. Lean, flat organizations with minimal layers have responded well to swiftly change and adopted the new front. Corporates with dominant teams with little empowerment to employees had a difficult time to adopt.'

Shridhar Narayan

'I believe in the inverted pyramid framework of leadership. This is rooted in the management philosophy of servant leadership, which was coined by Robert Greenleaf. A servant leader primarily focuses on the growth and well-being of people and the communities to which they belong. While a traditional leader generally exercises power by being at the top of the pyramid, servant leaders share power, by putting the needs of others first, helping them develop and perform as highly as possible. Servant leadership is about empowering team members and upending the traditional leadership pyramid, thereby giving all team members a sense of ownership in the organization. The main task of a leader is to make his/her job inconsequential. They should serve by creating a space where individual voices can grow and be heard, and where fear-based leadership is overcome.'

Dilip Pal

'Leaders need to set clear direction and goals and encourage a greater degree of empowerment in order to succeed in this new era. Employees will not be able to perform their roles without being fully empowered.'

With a safe atmosphere, empowered teams and matrix working, we need every individual to feel confident and demonstrate self-efficacy. Let us explore how we can embrace self-efficacy in our day-to-day lives.

14

Self-Efficacy

John was leading the global finance operations for a company in Seattle. He had to set up the finance back office for the company and they zeroed in on Manila as the location. Robin was a qualified accountant, working as a sales controller in Manila. He was analytical, hard-working and always produced results. When John was looking for a shared service head, the leadership team in Philippines recommended Robin. John liked the idea of promoting internal talent, and everyone seemed happy as Robin was considered knowledgeable, collaborative, easy to approach and friendly.

For Robin, the new role was like charting unknown territory. Moving away from business controlling to back office seemed like a step backwards, however, he realized it would give him a great opportunity to lead a large team, so he accepted it.

Under Robin's leadership, the centre started growing. However, one key challenge was to attract new talent and retain employees. Attrition was high at over 40 per cent in a few months, causing major issues in delivery of services. Initial reports suggested that the problem might be that other shared services in Manila were paying much higher salaries than they were, so John took all possible measures such as increasing salaries, awarding extra bonuses, and starting recognition and training programmes, but nothing seemed to stem the flow of people.

John realized that the reason must be beyond money and decided to visit the centre. That was when he found a demotivated team. John had one-on-one discussions with Robin's team members, and the common perception was that while Robin was a great person, he was not a great leader. While he knew his own job, he was not confident about taking decisions and avoided tough conversations. The team felt that it was due to Robin's weak leadership that people were leaving, which was causing more stress and overwork for everyone who remained. Thus, there was a vicious circle causing damage to the company.

John was still hopeful about Robin and decided to be his mentor. Robin agreed. John first identified the real issue, which was about developing self-efficacy in Robin and in his team. As Robin was open to feedback, willing to change and put in significant effort, progress was visible in a short time.

Self-efficacy is not only about having knowledge or confidence about a topic or in general; it is the ability to demonstrate that knowledge or confidence and to lead through that trait. People often confuse confidence with self-efficacy. A person acquires confidence through experience, knowledge, education, upbringing and other social or emotional factors. However, having confidence does not make everyone a great leader. That takes self-efficacy. As psychologist Albert Bandura said, 'Self-efficacy is the belief in one's ability to influence events that effect one's life and control over the way these events are experienced.'

Experience, past success, life events and perceived social acceptance are some of the major factors that affect self-efficacy. It is proven that people with higher self-efficacy can be decisive and confident about making things happen. All of us react in different ways when under stress, as discussed in the chapter on emotional resilience. And the ability to handle such situations in a calm and mature way often tells us the level of self-efficacy in a leader. A team or leader with high self-efficacy plans better, prepares carefully for a task, is more professional in their approach to tackling problems, avoids erratic or unprofessional behaviour, owns a problem, and reaches out to people for help to solve an issue. Taking failure as a learning and not going into a negative spiral is a crucial part of it.

Leaders with self-efficacy are positive leaders who are willing to walk the extra mile, while people with low self-efficacy tend to avoid new challenges and be averse to any sort of risk-taking.

As a new-age leader, it is not only important to demonstrate this quality, it is equally important to develop a team that thrives on it too. A word of caution, though: be mindful of people who are shallow in their confidence. Being high on self-efficacy without proper content knowledge is harmful to an organization as such people may end up failing due to their overestimation of their own abilities.

Following are a few tips on how we can develop a team with high self-efficacy.

Value each team member as they are

Everyone is different. Everyone has unique strengths, weaknesses and needs. As a leader, if you want to promote self-efficacy, you need to understand what makes a person successful, what values he or she believes in, their ambitions, and how can you build on his or her strengths. As a leader, ensure the role you assign suits the person's abilities. Everyone has something to contribute; you need to leverage and multiply that contribution by building on strengths.

Appreciate new ideas

A person with self-efficacy is not shy to bring new ideas to the table, however, he or she will stop doing so unless they are accepted and encouraged. As a leader, you need to ensure that you value those ideas, and no one is judged if their ideas are not suitable and not finally implemented. Encourage conversation by asking open-ended questions.

Stand up for your team

There are many ways by which you can make your team feel confident. We have already spoken about psychological safety, which is one of the critical elements to building confidence in your team members. One thing is certain: the best thing you can do to make your team confident is stand up for them and support them when they need you the most.

Show gratitude

Appreciation always works if you want to build self-efficacy in your team. We humans, at any stage of life or career, like to be acknowledged for what we are and what we have achieved. As a leader, ensure that you appreciate the work done by each member as needed. I have seen many leaders hesitate to show appreciation or gratitude, but when we need to build self-efficacy, it is one of our most effective tools. Let everyone know that you appreciate your colleagues' efforts as it will be a great motivator to build confidence.

Offer new learning opportunities

A continuous development culture helps people gain knowledge, which makes them feel more competent. And competency helps build self-efficacy. As a leader, ensure your team members continuously upgrade their skills and remain relevant in the market. For example, with new technologies being invented every day, anyone who does not update or upgrade themselves cannot remain confident in the new world. Ensure your team members get exposure beyond their regular scope of work, and put them into cross-functional teams giving them an opportunity to work on projects not directly related to their strengths and knowledge, and various management-development programmes to build all-round personality, which will lead to self-efficacy.

Delegate

Most ambitious people would love to step into the boss's shoes sooner rather than later. Most would like to do the work that their manager is supposed to perform. With this in mind, decide what you can delegate to enhance competency in your team. Delegation is an art and a subject in itself, and we won't go into too much detail here. However, to develop self-efficacy in your team, you need to understand what, when and to whom to delegate based on the skill set and aptitude of a person. Hand-hold them as needed and help them build competency, and in turn, confidence.

SELF-EFFICACY VOICES

Prriti Narain

'Self-belief is always an important trait! In an uncertain world where everything around us is changing, it is even more so. Alongside self-efficacy is also self-awareness. Being realistic about our strengths and weaknesses helps us grow constantly. If we have too much of one or the other, we will start feeling the effects of either narcissism or anxiety or other disorders. Balance is the key.'

Soumen Mukherjee

'Training our minds and psyches to absorb multidimensional information and the ability to leverage the power of information will be a skill with no alternatives in the digital world, helping us to develop self-efficacy as a leadership trait.'

Surajit Banerjee

'The uncertainty of the economic world will require all effort to be concentrated on building individual self-efficacy through a regulated programme completely focused on outcomes, with a graded approach to complexity of achievement.'

Monideepa Bhattacharya

'Self-efficacy has been gaining momentum as a thematic discussion personally as well as professionally. With growing uncertainties and the stark reminder of our mortality, the COVID-19 pandemic is teaching us that the only way we can survive and even thrive is to believe—in self, most importantly.'

Anushree Singh

'Self-efficacy is an important trait as it is our own belief in our abilities that allows us to deliver high performance. To be successful in life, the first step is to believe you have it in yourself to accomplish something. If that is absent, no matter how much we train, coach or empower, it will be a lost battle. And during difficult times, this will only become more pronounced.'

Subodh Dubey

'We are living in unprecedented and difficult times, and in such times, an individual's belief and action that is driven from his or her confidence is essential. Self-efficacy will remain an important trait for the future.'

Dilip Pal

'There is no better time than now to put to test the self-efficacy of employees in order to deal with the situation without being overwhelmed. The confidence to deal with such situations also comes from personal experience. While no one has seen or dealt with a pandemic or crisis of this magnitude before, many of us have gone through some form of challenges in our lives. By reflecting on those challenges, it is possible to apply those learnings to today's situation.'

Great leaders are known for crisis management. But the virtual, interconnected world changes the whole dynamic in times of crisis. Let us look at how crisis management now needs to be different from what it was in the past.

15

Crisis Leadership

It is often assumed that a leader should be able to manage a crisis, that this is the true litmus test.

I often wonder: How equipped are we as leaders in the face of a crisis? Phenomena like COVID-19, in which the entire world stops functioning, may be rare. This is an unprecedented situation, and most of us were not ready for it. Fair enough. But it is also true that crises usually don't provide us with advance notice to prepare, and we seldom know when they will end. These are the times that expose the vulnerability of most leaders, and the leaders who show their resilience and emerge as winners are true heroes.

Indeed, we *have* seen heroes across every organization in recent times. How did these people learn to manage a crisis better than others? Should we make it a mandatory skill for all leaders to learn?

In the last thirty years, we have faced multiple crises. To name a few, in the 1990s, the world saw economic and financial crises in India, Mexico, Russia and Ecuador; the Asian financial crisis; and the Swedish banking crisis. The 2000s started with the dotcom bubble bursting, followed by the 9/11 attacks in the US; the economic, financial and banking crises in Turkey, Uruguay, Ireland, Venezuela and Spain; and the housing crisis in the US. The 2010s brought us the European sovereign debt crisis; the Chinese stock market crash; and the economic, financial and banking crises in Portugal, Venezuela, Russia and Turkey.

There have also been local disasters such as terrorist attacks, protests, floods and hurricanes. Organization-specific incidences are also constant, such as the loss of a big customer, the mass exodus of employees, cash crunches, strikes or similar.

You may ask: all these situations occurred in the past and great leaders have handled them well. What makes the future any different?

The most significant change is that we are now dealing with crises in a connected world, and this has brought with it many challenges as news flows much faster than ever before, local agitations can quickly take a global shape, people's voices can be heard and seen more easily, and obviously, we can't rule out the impact of fake news that is seeping into our everyday lives through social media.

We do not need another COVID-19 to learn how to manage a crisis; any of these more common situations also change the way we plan as organizations because, in simple terms, they alter the demand–supply equation, leading to uncertainty. While some industries do benefit from these crises, most do suffer. Whether there is higher or lower demand, a leader needs to carefully steer through the complicated terrain, riddled with potential landmines.

As management styles are changing and layers in the organizations are getting leaner, another question may arise: is it the job of only senior leaders in the organization to steer the company through a crisis? The answer is a clear no, and hence let us look at what we can all master to lead through a crisis. And we'll do it through a story again to drive home a few points.

The year was 2007, and Sharon was regional head of a consumer durables company based in Singapore. An avid reader with a keen interest in world economics, Sharon had a good hunch about the future of economies. Consumer goods prices were falling, and market conditions were tense as every player fought for market share. In one of her company's all-employee meetings, Sharon spoke about the fact that a recession might hit the market. Some believed her, others did not.

'The world is going to change,' she said. 'I want to be future-secured, I do not want to fight for market share now. Instead, I will take the prices up, and if that means I lose some market share, so be it. For the next few months, I want you to concentrate on programmes to reduce the cost of our products. This will widen the gap between my selling price and cost, and we will make more profit per machine.'

Some of her colleagues laughed. 'Sharon, it's simple math,' they said. 'I agree our per-machine profit will be higher, but it is of no use as, in total, we will lose more money with lower volume.'

Sharon agreed with the math but disagreed with the reasoning. 'In the short term, due to the recession, the demand is going to fall for all manufacturers. But once the recession is over, which I expect in about two years, demand will be back. And by then we will have already established our higher price points, and we will have a lower cost.'

They finally began to see the logic. 'Don't compromise on the quality of our product by cutting any corners,' she warned. 'Our customers are used to our quality, I do not want to fool them. I want to make much more money over the next many years at the cost of short-term losses.'

The organization indeed embarked on this strategy, and in a few years not only did profits triple, but they also gained substantial market share due to sustained quality.

I met Sharon a couple of years ago and asked her to share a few learnings from those days. 'I wanted to take advantage of the crisis. I had to take some decisions that were not traditional. I relied on the available data, involved my whole organization to tide over the situation and, as a leader, I remained positive,' she explained. 'One more thing: I missed no opportunity to share the lessons learnt during this crisis widely. Who knows, they may come in handy in the future so we can all be better prepared.'

Let me elaborate on a few points from Sharon's story.

Don't panic, stay positive

Every crisis is an opportunity. The old saying 'every cloud has a silver lining' holds especially true during a crisis. Many leaders look for opportunities and work on these during the crisis, so after it all blows over, the organization can benefit from it.

This is not the time to get overwhelmed. I am not suggesting you remain positive for the sake of it, but rather work on future opportunities during the time of crisis to ensure that the organization can ride on that wave when the crisis ends. Positivity spreads, and a positive leader can spread positivity among employees, rather than focusing on doomsday scenarios and how the crisis will end the organization if not the world.

Communicate to manage chaos

In a state of crisis, when the future is uncertain, chaos will creep in and cause unproductive emotions, fear and conflict, leading to stress and a decline in productive output. As a leader, you need to communicate from the front and stop the spread of panic. And if this means you need to over-communicate, so be it.

Be adaptive

A leader needs to look at the situation and adapt as needed. A crisis can come from any front. It might be caused by internal issues such as product failure, a strike, a cash-flow shortage or similar. Or it could be led by external factors such as COVID-19 or an economic crisis. One formula won't solve all issues, and a leader needs to ensure he or she listens to all signals, analyses the possible outcomes, remains agile and adapts to the needs of the situation as required.

Do not shake the foundational principles

Every organization is built on values and foundational principles. A crisis may shake those foundations and push the leader to take decisions that do not support core values. Here's where leadership comes in: a leader should not be shaken, but rather should adhere to what the organization is built for. A crisis gives us the opportunity to act together, forgetting our differences, and a leader needs to facilitate that.

Lead with your heart

A crisis sometimes leads to positive outcomes, but in the short term, many organizations will face adversity such as the loss of jobs, supply issues for customers, cash flow shortages, lower profits, and many more.

Thus, while leaders need to ensure that organizations ride out a crisis, at the same time they need to handle the people around them with care. For example, even if the outcome of a conversation may not be good for an employee about to lose a job, there are many ways to handle it. A leader needs to show care and respect even when delivering such news, and that will create the culture of the organization and can also motivate many others to hold on during a time of crisis. Honesty pays, so share as much as you know and be realistic and authentic in every action and word you speak. This is the time your team will look to you: stand by them.

Trust

This word appears across different leadership traits, and crisis leadership too leans on trust as a foundational factor. Trust is not only about trusting employees, it is also about showing your stakeholders, society and customers that *they* can trust *you*. And that is only possible through actions and conversations that demonstrate that the core principles are being upheld by your organization even in a time of crisis.

Take decisions

A leader needs to take decisions that others fear to take; that is one of the roles of a leader especially when life is not as usual. There will be times when we need to take decisions on issues we've never faced before, and as a leader we can't avoid them. Rely as much as possible on data and experience, call in experts, and get help from others as crises call for a different way of dealing with situations. Great leaders are masters at separating emotions from practical matters and they never take any outcome personally.

Rely on data, not rumours

These days, it is not easy to differentiate between real news and fake news. It is scary how fake news is packaged and spread, and people often take it as authentic. This is affecting not only individuals but also organizations, as such manufactured news affects all kinds of sentiment. You can't control the spread of such news, but you can control the damage if you do not succumb to pressure created by rumours and rely on data to ensure reality reaches your stakeholders, customers and employees.

Involve people to share ownership

You are not alone, so avoid trying to solve issues by yourself. When the problem is shared, it becomes everyone's problem, and not only that of the leader. This is how you can secure participation from others in the organization, and the power of a team is always more than the power of an individual.

CRISIS LEADERSHIP VOICES

Haresh Hemrajani

'Corporates have recognized the power of social media to attract and retain their employees, customers and prospects. However, very few have embraced the power of social media to respond and perform actionable alerts.

'With the onset of COVID-19, leaders have realized the importance of faster decision-making and ensuring swift, accurate communication during a crisis. It is important to base decisions on diverse sources and this is where AI/social media can play a vital role. The use of AI tools to sort through rich data from social media, internal wikis or helpdesk systems can provide actionable alerts. The ability to react in a timely manner and contain or manage situations affecting the corporate brand and specific customer service challenges will pay significant dividends.'

Shyam Mamidi

'At the time of crisis, leadership behaviours come to the forefront to drive the objectives of the organization. Most organizations are expected to display leadership behaviours which empathize and lay more trust on the employees and to empower them; create a culture of innovation within the organizations where employees and other stakeholders could voice their ideas which are acknowledged, valued and incorporated into the products and services of the corporates. This is how the new ecosystems, new revenue streams from new business models will get created since the ecosystem would more likely provide a greater overall value than individual organization in the network. Those leaders who democratize, engage, empower and encourage their employees are likely to be always surrounded with ideas and energy as compared to the ones who have the authoritative or autocratic approach. Various factors such as financial reserves and cash, are always important, keeping them away, the resiliency with employees and clients come from how much value is being generated through the transactions between the two organizations. Hence, in crisis, it is important to understand the value generated to client not only in terms of dollars, but also in terms of end-to-end customer experience.'

Dhiren Kinger

'Crises can distract us when coupled with too much information. The leader of 2025 will be required to have the calmness and stability to be able to focus on the vision that the company wants to achieve and not get overwhelmed in a crisis. The future leader will have to develop a bifocal vision that not only focuses on the long-term, but takes care of short-term distractions and challenges as well.'

Diptendu Mondal

'It is felt that the less we need to engage in crisis management, the better it is for the organization. However, it is next to impossible to avoid all crises indefinitely. COVID-19 has showed us how we should be prepared to handle these sorts of emergencies, specifically when we are not physically present together.

'The world is moving very fast. In today's scenario, what was normal yesterday is perceived to be a crisis today as expectations of turn-around time for response and resolution have changed exponentially. With technology changing in no time, organizations must act fast to adapt.'

Sameer Agarwal

'The new-age data revolution or industry evolution 4.0 and the pandemic have brought VUCA (volatility, uncertainty, complexity and ambiguity) to reality, and events like demonetization and GST implementation have ensured that crisis leadership is no longer a specialized skill but a necessary one. This skill enables leaders to rewrite and quickly execute ever-changing business continuity plans and risk matrix, and continuously look for opportunities to grow organically and inorganically to continue to be relevant in a dynamic geopolitical and economic landscape Crisis leadership helps steady the various stakeholders and enables transparent communication and action plans, which ensures that there is no crash landing.'

Satyakam Basu

'The new world will be led by people who are change agents themselves and have been riding the crest of continuous evolution and innovation. They need to be at the forefront of all the innovations and be able to percolate them down to their teams by personal example.

'Being able to anticipate changes and the concomitant disruptions they bring, and the ability to successfully mitigate these disruptions will be the hallmark of the new leader. The ability to convert every such change or disruption into an opportunity will be the essential demand from new leaders, and only if they are able to do this will the team accept them as leaders. Because hierarchical management structures will yield place to flatter organizations, leaders won't be able to hide behind anything and will be under constant focus to navigate from one change to another and another. People who are able to do this will endure as leaders.'

Subodh Dubey

'One of the top qualities of a good leader is to be resilient. A good leader should appreciate the harsh realities of life and inspire people to see the power to pass through the crisis, and take actions.

'I want to give an example of my experience with the CEO of one of the companies where I worked.

'The company was going through a serious business turmoil, and to reduce cost, reduction in manpower was the prime action as per their strategy. The way the CEO managed the whole process by personally helping his team to get another assignment in other companies was actually leading by example. He mentioned in one of the meetings, "I had to take tough decisions, but we all should understand the crisis, and that we need to act with patience and take the best possible approach."'

Indraneel Roy Choudhury

'The COVID-19 crisis has made the world more polarized and there are geopolitical developments arising every day. Social media and AI are important and can be harnessed by leaders for the greater good of all, whether it is an organization, institution or country. Subjectivity and uncertainty will be the cornerstones of that world, hence the challenge for future leaders will be to think long-term and ensure sustainability.'

With so much change, people will need someone to confide in and talk to. Coaching and mentoring will hence be useful as tools for future leadership. Let us investigate the huge possibility that exists for leaders who learn to coach and mentor.

16

Coaching and Mentoring

Managers often consider themselves to be coaches, but I wonder if they really understand the essence of coaching. While some may be naturally great at it, some, I will argue, are not, as coaching is a skill one needs to learn.

With coaching as a profession still evolving, most organizations are hiring external professional coaches to help their senior leaders tide over certain situations. The culture of coaching still hasn't spread deep into organizations, with few actually supporting their mid- or entry-level managers with a coach. It is still considered a luxury by most organizations and often used only to develop top talent or senior management.

Coaching in the future won't be seen just as interim help for someone who needs development, but as an effective tool for an engaged team. We certainly need more coaches embedded in the system as the need for coaching skills is growing. Over time, I won't be surprised if most of us need to learn how to coach irrespective of our level in the workplace, as organizations come to expect their employees to at least have an understanding of the art of coaching. It will be essential for each leader or aspiring leaders as organizations incorporate coaching as a core thought for managing teams.

I myself am a professionally certified coach. I attained this degree as I felt the need to become a coach when I started handling a large team spread across the world. The virtual world and new-age professionals demanded that I develop coaching skills. Let me share a story that inspired me to be a coach and think like a coach all the time.

Indranil moved to Europe a few years ago after a successful career in Asia. He had employed a directional style of leadership over the years, telling his people what to do, and they delivered what he wanted to achieve. He was successful and grew well in his corporate career, which led to his global job based in Paris.

In his new role, he started leading global teams. But even as he was delivering results, he started losing talent, and over the next six months, seven out of the fifteen people in his team resigned. Indranil was surprised: he had always been known as a people's manager and had never faced such an exodus before. When he asked his people why they were leaving, they all said they wanted to pursue other opportunities for growth, a typical non-controversial answer that we often get during exit interviews. Indranil accepted the logic and hired new people for those positions. However, attrition continued.

During his annual appraisal, Indranil's French boss gave him the feedback that he needed to change his management style to one that was more collaborative and inclusive; that he needed to listen to people, align with the team and take them along on the journey and be less directional.

Indranil had always been a great learner who accepted feedback as a gift, so he spoke to his team and did a 360-degree assessment wherein it became clear that people found him too directional and task-driven, and felt that he lacked listening skills—that he was always ready with a solution even before the start of a conversation.

This was hard feedback to hear. Indranil was concerned as he had always felt quite proud of the leadership style that had made him successful over the years. He realized that he needed a structured intervention, and he appointed a coach to help him through the situation. It took him a few months to figure out the issues that he needed to address, after which he had to master a few skills essential in today's changing world, one of them being coaching skills. This process helped him remain relevant.

Let me share a few tips for effective coaching that can help everyone remain in coaching mode while leading.

Remain curious

A leader who is also a coach shows the curiosity to explore more before arriving at a conclusion. Don't rush to drive home a point without exploring possibilities.

Curiosity is the difference between knowing and discovering. Curiosity keeps judgement at bay and encourages different considerations and inclusions. We humans are born curious, and hence as children we ask many questions, but over time our education system forces us to suppress our curiosity in favour of efficiency. The time has come to be that child in order to explore the unknown.

Don't be directional

In a coaching conversation, a leader doesn't direct the employees on what to do. Instead, the team discusses a job at hand. They then reach an agreement on how to proceed, in which the objective is no more solely owned by the leader, but has become a joint objective. Through this process, both the manager and the employee agree on how to achieve the goal, and the employee leads the way to discover the path while the manager facilitates the journey.

Listen actively

The manager listens with all his mind and heart—the coach inside the manager is mentally present during the entire conversation. Listening is the core of coaching. The manager needs to focus on the person on the other side and capture all the information being thrown at him or her, be it verbal or nonverbal. It is all about making the other person believe that there is nothing more important in this world than them, and that the manager is listening to actually understand and not just for the sake of it.

Ask clarifying questions

A coach asks clarifying questions to get to the heart of an issue instead of directly arriving at a solution. The questions are often simple but encourage the other person to elaborate on matters, bringing previously unstated issues to the fore. A leader in coach mode needs to learn to ask open-ended questions and ensure that the conversation starts, not ends even before being explored. The simple practice of driving a conversation with the words 'what', 'how', 'when' and 'where' can work wonders.

Ensure accountability

A coaching conversation always ends with forwarding actions and ensuring that accountability is accepted and owned by the employee. At the end of such conversations, the next steps are established, which makes the discussion effective.

Be empathetic

It is a word often spoken, but not always understood or practised. Empathy is all about connecting without judgement and trying to understand a situation or a person's perspective without being directional or driving a personal agenda. This quality helps leaders connect with the team, ensuring their support even through difficult decisions or changes. Empathy builds trust, which a leader needs to have from his or her team at every step. In the current world, the organization expects each leader to lead with empathy.

COACHING AND MENTORING VOICES

Prriti Narain

'The world as we knew it changed almost overnight. Such a rapid change, along with personal and professional losses and looming uncertainty for a prolonged period, can be harsh. Mental health experts tell us that after the COVID-19 pandemic, there will be a mental health pandemic. Support during such times is imperative. Depending on the situation and individual needs, seeking help is relevant for each one of us.

'Coaching helps provide an unbiased perspective. Those looking for coaching should embark on this journey with clear end objectives to help identify the right coach as well as keep both the coach and you focused on what you want to achieve.'

Shridhar Narayan

'In my new avatar of being a mentor for various start-ups, where I am working with a different generation of people who are more technology-driven, I have realized that there has to be greater delegation and decision-making at all levels. In this digital era, one has to be more of an influencer and move from having a task-oriented approach to being a people-oriented leader.

'A good manager will realize that leadership affects employee behaviour. There is a great focus on individuality amongst working professionals. Everyone wants to work in their own way, and therefore modulating the style of interaction and the manner of management from person to person will be the key to becoming a successful leader.'

Dr P.V. Ramana Murthy

'Leaders will need to be more open, humble and authentic than ever before. Servant leadership will gain more and more strength as the workforce becomes laden with the younger generation that will not defer to power and authority but will care for an unified purpose. As leaders, we need coach and mentor the next generation into this way of thinking in a non-threatening manner.'

Himal Tiwari

'Career management and growth will largely be self-driven, but we will see new formal and informal methods of sponsorship and development. The more formal methodology of learning is likely to be challenged, as it is unlikely to connect well with this new reality. New coaching methodologies will emerge and you're likely to go back to creating direct coaching methodology as in high-performance sports … New leaders will embrace, promote and encourage higher purpose versus higher performance. This will involve connecting with the employee in a different engagement model that is almost a mix of parent, teacher, coach and friend!'

Surajit Banerjee

'Coaching will move towards more scenario-building and away from past experiences, as behavioural events may become less predictive of the new normal expectations. However, its relevance can hardly be overemphasized. It will be a new world for coaches who will need to assist in building new paradigms for their coachees.'

Naveen Begwani

'With these evolving times, the role of a leader is also undergoing a transformation. There are far more challenges than that existed just even a year ago. Not only does he or she have to manage his or her business in the tough economic scenario and be answerable to the stakeholders, they are also expected to continue to coach and mentor their team. They are expected to lead, share a common vision, manage performance, and upskill and develop the team—remotely. This means a new paradigm of thinking and approach, and the need for coaching and mentoring in the virtual world.'

Puneet Gupta

'It's the age to be the coach and not the boss. With new-age talents, respect will not be bestowed upon you based on your age, experience or level, but on your performance/conduct with each employee. Can't take it for granted, got to earn it every single day, unlike today where one can get through for years because one is the boss. Talents will appreciate mentors and coaches more than the people who like to demonstrate authority.'

Shyam Mamidi

'Coaching will be a constant need, with experience and idea-sharing leading to key innovations. Coaching as a trait is in-built for those who have a lot of interest and compassion or self-commitment to see their teams grow. As coaches, it is important to have the right climate of learning within the organization or teams. The teams should feel the supportive, compassionate, safe and transparent culture wherein their ideas and work resonate and are acknowledged. A culture that magnifies the little steps of success and diminishes the errors during the attempts to innovate or deliver.'

Monideepa Bhattacharya

'Every individual during the pandemic has had a unique experience—the social, economic, political and mental implications of a black swan event have been pervasive and yet individual. Coaching is going to be an essential organizational trait going forward, and possibly even outside of it, as is evidenced by the spurt in freelance coaches during this time. With rising economic anxieties and uncertainties, the changing face of "normal" and the pressures of reinvention, coaches will play a significant role in helping people navigate this crisis and continue to thrive in their personal and professional lives.'

Subodh Dubey

'There will be after-effects of the pandemic in terms of health, economy and other unprecedented challenges, and coaching can definitely help cope with these.'

Dilip Pal

'Coaching will be an important leadership tool in the new era. Work-from-home will result in employees being separated physically from their colleagues and normal workplaces. Remotely touching base with those who they used to see regularly will not be as satisfying, leading to a feeling of being lost. Leaders will have to step up and master the art of coaching to help employees get through this crisis.'

Anushree Singh

'COVID-19 has left managers unprepared and in situations for which they have no references. Coaching teaches leaders and people managers to manage the pace of change and come up with creative solutions, drive performance through virtual teams, engage teams, lead through crises, balance being demanding with empathy, cultivate a digital mindset and drive effectiveness, and build trust while remote working.'

SECTION 3

Future-Proofing

In the last few chapters, we have spoken about the different needs of leadership in the future. We've read many stories and comments from industry leaders. As many of these behaviours or traits are overlapping, I want to remove any confusion in readers' minds by summarizing how one can inculcate the winning leadership traits emerging from our discussion.

There are three distinct categories of leadership that will emerge over time, and all the traits our future leaders need come under them. They are all of equal importance, and an ideal leader will be one who has internalized a blend of all these traits, manifested through three main approaches:

Leading through technology

These are the leaders who embrace technology as part of their lives; who look beyond today towards future possibilities; the visionaries. People look up to them for their futuristic thinking. Such leaders aim to automate mundane work and look at technology to make life interesting. They work to ensure our workforce uses its intellect effectively, and adds value to the work instead of running processes that can be done through machines. These are the leaders who will create opportunities and the aspiration in people to think ahead and grow.

Leading through processes

These are the leaders who are process-driven, disciplined and structured; who can make complex problems simple and provide solutions. They are revered for their ways of working and the way they simplify, standardize and systemize processes. These leaders facilitate delegation and decision-making at all levels of an organization, keeping control through processes.

Leading from the heart

These are the leaders who put a person before a task; visibly care about others; show leadership driven from their hearts beyond the call of regular duty; care about the development of the team; do not judge people for their shortcomings; coach their teams and help them develop.

We need to have a mix of these qualities in order to adapt to the future of leadership. Let us look at them in more detail.

17

Leading through Technology

Remain contemporary, remain relevant

I've known Vishan, the finance director of a large service organization based in Bengaluru, for many years. Last year when I visited him, he told me he had enrolled in a six-week course on the technological trends affecting the finance world. I was surprised because as far as I knew, technology had never been his area of interest. And then he told me the story of his career.

'I've been in the corporate world for the past twenty-five years and every organization I have worked for has considered me a top talent. To be honest, I became a finance professional by chance, as my family was pressuring me to pursue a secure career; I had no interest in the finance world. My real interest was always in knowing human behaviour, and in hindsight I think I should have joined human resources.

'My father wanted me to become a chartered accountant. I took the exams and cleared them in my first attempt. It seemed to me that the industry was waiting for me, and I started enjoying my corporate success. In fact, I grew faster than many of my colleagues.

'In my spare time, I continued my development in the area of people skills, which I believe was one of the primary reasons for my success. I led people with passion and my seniors always appreciated my leadership skills.

'Till now my journey has been great, but with so much technological change and the possibility to simplify and standardize my team's work, I sometimes feel outdated, hollow. I need to know more. I can't have meaningful conversations with my team as I do not have much knowledge of the changing landscape of systems and technology. And now I realize if I do not invest in myself, in learning and exploring the technological trends, soon my organization will have no need for me, and I will be left behind. I need to outskill to remain contemporary, to remain relevant.'

Leadership seldom had a need to be clued in to technology in the past; it was considered the domain of specialized departments. I believe the world is no longer moving in the same direction: technological advances will dictate the new world and as a future leader, one needs to be aware of what is happening and know how to guide the organization to take the next steps. I am not advising all leaders to become experts on technology, but in the future, everyone will need to be *savvy* about technology. I have always joked, the senior-most leaders get the best laptops, mostly to use email, Excel and PowerPoint. But this is no longer enough. We need to invest time in learning about technological developments and encourage our teams to keep learning too in order to lead a technology-enabled organization. Let us expand our horizons by not staying confined to our area of work and keeping an eye on the developments in the outside world, in the technology-led future.

Encourage data to lead

Robert is the general manager for a manufacturing unit in Vietnam. This is the story he told me:

'Every year, my team and I spend at least three months preparing the annual plan. I have always believed that investing time at an early juncture helps us execute the next year well. We have enough in-house experience, and we believed we knew the market well. Thus, building a few scenarios from our experience, deciding on required investments and thinking about competitive actions was not that difficult.

'I was aware of a new global CEO joining us and had heard he was extremely sharp and data-driven. While he had the reputation of being a straight talker, some of his close associates also felt he could be rude. Someone said he was allergic to "guesses".

'Before my first presentation to him, I was somewhat sceptical, but also confident since I had been following the same process for the past many years. I opened the discussion with some basic economic data, market projections that I had gathered from my team, validated by experience and judgement. After a few minutes, he stopped the meeting. "Robert, I do not want to hear what you think, I want you to tell me what the data thinks," he said. "I believe in you, but I believe in data more than you. So, let's stop the meeting and we'll reassemble in a few weeks when you are ready. In the meanwhile, stop doing the thinking that a machine can do for you and start leading the way a human needs to lead. That is your job."

'I was offended and humiliated. No one had ever spoken to me like that before, but then I realized that what he was trying to do was drive a cultural change through the company.'

Contrary to popular belief, many organizations are miles away from being data driven; decisions are still taken based on hearsay, feelings, experience and intuition. With data and information being readily available, should we not change our decision-making processes?

A data-driven culture calls for a mindset change, and the tone has to be set at the top. This is an important leadership quality we all need to pick up to ensure our organizations rely on proper data and analysis and not on rumours or guesswork. We need to make data-driven analysis a fundamental requirement to lead, which will change the whole perspective of the organization. However, be mindful of analysis paralysis and data overload to avoid procrastination. Understanding what is needed and what can be ignored or discarded will be an important leadership trait.

Create a niche

I was chatting with my friend Roland, who leads the finance team of a large global organization based in the Netherlands, and our discussion the other day provided me clarity on the need to be tech savvy in every domain.

'I am noticing a huge change in the skill sets we require. Before, as I moved through the corporate world, I was supposed to know almost everything that was happening in the finance world. When I started leading a team as the country finance director for Germany, all aspects of finance reported to me. All the activities were performed in the country, and I had a large team around me. This made me learn many things, but nothing in depth. I was Jack of all trades, master of none. Nothing wrong in that. But over the past few years, I have noticed a huge transformation in the finance world, with many of the jobs moving out of their home countries and functioning remotely. Today, I recruit people who have much more in-depth knowledge in the areas they are handling, be it functional or technical knowledge. I need more specialists than generalists. I don't think I would have survived in the new world with the skill sets I came to the industry with. Now you need to have a niche, be a specialist in some area.'

For many years we have survived by being generalists without a specific niche, and many of us have excelled in our careers. In the past, organizations needed such skills. The time has now come for specialism, especially at the junior- and mid-levels. We all must have something in our kitties that sets us apart, and technology can help us achieve this. As leaders, we need to encourage this in our people and help them grow in their areas of interest, too. The idea of fixed, rigid job functions has been changing, and will continue to shift. To be considered a talent and grow in an organization, one needs to offer some unique skill or capability, and the need for generalists will diminish.

Ensure technological competence in all teams

Colin, the information management head of a family-based organization headquartered in Zurich, shared a story that gave me an insight into why diverse thinking can work so well.

'My team is always full of techies. Very brainy people completely hooked on to systems all the time. Over the last few years, we have started using six sigma methodology which was the logical move to drive the continuous improvement projects. Now I have also included talents from other academic backgrounds such as lawyers and finance professionals. There are even two young management trainees in my team. This gives a range of experience to the group.

'People thought I was mad when I initiated this idea. But what I find now is that diverse ideas are being embraced; healthy challenges are being thrown at each other during my team meetings. The experienced people are learning from the youngsters about the latest trends in technology and the social environment; finance professionals are teaching techies how to save costs; lawyers are keeping us within the boundaries of our legal remit; youngsters are learning management practices from experienced leaders. Overall, it's a perfect mix, and when I need more knowledge, I pull others in on a temporary basis.'

Indeed a great, bold idea. Collaboration and knowledge-sharing will be increasingly important as people work together in the new world, be it physically or virtually. And to facilitate that, leaders need to put together a diverse team. Research has shown that diverse teams excel; and while this has always been true, it will become even more evident as we move into the virtual world with more distance working. Complementary skills will be essential for cross-functional collaboration and agile working, while allowing us to remain objective and consider more possibilities. It will help keep the focus on facts while exploring more areas, and then deciding on a path. Innovation takes a front seat when you are pooling knowledge from different parts of the organization; as a whole, we get intellectually enriched. Technology will lead the way we work in the future and influence most decisions, which is why many leaders believe that having technical knowledge in every team will enhance the team capability manifold.

18

Leading through Processes

Clear, simple steps

Here is a story that Aditya, head of payables of a large corporation, shared with me recently.

'I have always been known as an intuitive manager, and I took a lot of pride in that. People always said I have the ability to thrive in chaos and come up with a solution to a problem in no time.

'Then something changed over the last few years, I became stagnant in my career; the rapid growth I had experienced in the past stopped. When I spoke to my manager, he told me candidly that I had reached my peak, and beyond this point, I would be hitting my level of incompetence, and thus I would not grow further.

'I hated that conversation, got a bit emotional, but he did not change his mind. After a few weeks, I met my manager again, and he explained that he needed people with a process-oriented mind rather than experts in fixing problems. Again, the conversation did not go well, and we left our discussion in the middle. As I introspected further and spoke to a few others, I realized the need for a mindset shift. Later, my manager gave me a simple example that cleared my mind. He told me to study one of the global food giants. He told me to learn from them, how the process of producing burgers is defined centrally and how every outlet globally follows the process meticulously. No one can deviate and that is why the burgers taste almost the same in every outlet throughout the world.

'"This is the future," he said. "In times to come, processes will be defined by the global process-owners, and everyone will need to follow them. It is impossible to be successful if everyone defines their own process and thinks that's the best. You will still have problems and we will need intuitive managers like you to resolve issues, but that is not a career for the future. Leading through chaos will not be a preferred management style anymore, and you need to respect and adapt to that change."'

Process-driven organizations are the key to the future. As leaders, we need to learn and ensure that we drive such a culture in the organization. With data and information widely available, we need clear, simple processes to take the organization to the next level. Simplification is an art, and not everyone can do it. A process-driven leadership will call for leaders who can make complex issues simple through defined processes, and ensure that our teams make our organizations process-led rather than individual-led.

Rigorous governance

Eduardo leads the transformation team of a construction company based in Brazil. He was telling me how he noticed a clear difference between teams that have a strong sense of direction and those in which leaders do not take ownership of deliverables.

'Over the last few years, I have been leading the global transformation programme. Thanks to technology, I was able to automate most of the matrices, and the reporting of our progress has become quite transparent. Over the course of the transformation, we had weekly updates, and I ensured everyone was aware of the progress we were making. As a company, we believed in rigorous reviews and had a clear governance calendar in place. We also had the rigour of a two-day review meeting every quarter, face-to-face, at Sao Paolo, where all regional transformation leads participated and discussed progress with the top management.

'We did not stop our transformation programme during COVID-19; however, I realized two of my five regions were not progressing well and were short on delivery against the agreed savings target. While an initial review told me it was linked to the slowdown in the economy due to the pandemic, upon a deep dive I realized that the teams had stopped their established governance practices and reviews during the past few months. And the change in their behaviour was because they felt less pressured as the quarterly meeting had been called off due to the global restrictions in travel.

'I was extremely surprised, but it also taught me a few things. First of all, though I assumed everything was working well, the governance process had never been embedded and owned by the people. People adhered to it only because the head office wanted them to. Secondly, the quarterly face-to-face meeting was a kind of check for the team. They needed to face top management and wanted to look good, so they did their best to show progress. My biggest learning has been that remote working needs a very different governance model: you need to run the show almost like an aircraft where the pilot puts the aircraft on autopilot. And that calls for clear process and ownership.'

Distance working will create new challenges to keep everyone accountable for their commitments. This requires processes to define clear responsibility metrics, which are to be agreed upon by the relevant stakeholders. The future can't be left to faith and good intentions with people working remotely; we need to establish rigorous governance, predefine review meetings, and have clear performance indicators to hold people accountable and ensure no one can hide behind inefficiency.

Agility and adaptability

The story of Yvette may not be unique, but it makes the need for agility clearer.

'I have a few rules in life. I apply the same principles in my professional life as well. One of the rules I follow is: argue, fight, disagree as much as you want, but once agreed, just execute.

'It has worked for me. Throughout my career, before launching any new initiative, I have called for a two-day workshop in which I have included my stakeholders and project team. At the end of the workshop, we'd leave with a clear charter, project plan, stage gates, with governance fully defined. And from then onwards, the entire team would focus on execution. While I learnt the Deming cycle (Plan-Do-Check-Act) much earlier in my life and have applied it to every stage of a project, I was not adaptable to new ideas or processes after we agreed on a charter.

'However, over the past few years, I have had to change myself, as I realized I have been missing out on many opportunities. And the reason is simple: every day, technology is evolving, which gives us the opportunity to look at and solve issues differently. It has not been an easy transition for me, but I do not want to miss out anymore.'

No process can be set in stone; it requires constant updating and change. Being open to adapting is the rule of the game. Leaders of the future need to be agile and ensure any course correction that is required on the way is taken up.

End to end process-based organizations are here to stay, and the silo culture prevalent in many organizations will be replaced by more collaborative matrix ways of working. This calls for leaders who are agile, adaptable and can influence and facilitate decision-making. High interpersonal and influencing skills will be valued. Leaders need to have the courage and conviction to be open to ideas and feedback, encourage creativity, ensure course correction as needed, resolve differences, address conflicts, and define actions and next steps to move a team ahead.

19

Leading from the Heart

Demonstrate trust

I was talking to Simran, a new-age leader in her mid-career, about trust. She had a very interesting story to share from her own experience.

'A few months ago, my manager asked me to travel with her to our head office in New Delhi to make a presentation to the board of directors about an important project to be headed by her. "You will do the talking, I am there if you need any support," she said to me.

'I was surprised, since for my manager it should have been a big day, but instead, she told me to stand in. I think I did a good job as in the end, we got the approval to go ahead. I got tons of appreciation from the board members.

'In the evening, when we met to celebrate, I asked her why she had chosen me to present the project. "Fear is the greatest enemy of trust; I should take that away from my mind as well as from the minds of others. I just did that," she said with a smile. "When I was your age, I never got such an opportunity since my manager didn't give me such exposure. And now I realize it was because he feared my success would affect his career. These are great opportunities to develop leaders of the future, but he never had the courage to develop me, or give me more exposure than I'd had. In turn, he never earned that respect from me as a leader. I do not want to follow the same route. This was a great opportunity to show that I trust in your capability, and when you show someone that you trust them, seldom will he or she let you down."'

To Simran, this act of faith meant the world. 'I won't forget her or that day ever, as it was when I learnt how one can lead from the heart.'

Demonstrating trust in others and being trusted leads the list of priorities when one leads from the heart. Trust can't be gained just by talking about it; every action needs to be sincere and genuine, without any hidden agenda and with a respect for each other's viewpoint. This is the quality in human beings that is the foundation for long-lasting relationships.

In the past, we have seen many leaders with narcissistic traits, maintaining a larger-than-life image, keeping a certain distance from their team and caring too much about themselves. I am not sure if such leaders build trust in the team in the new world. The new-age leader needs to maintain close contact with the team and care about their well-being. 'You are important, how can I help you or how can I grow you?' should be their attitude. That should be their attitude towards others and instead of trying to project a larger than life personality, they need to be humble, honest, transparent and accessible.

Remain curious, encourage creativity

I was recently interviewing a young graduate from a reputed management institute. I was keen to have him on my team but was aware that it wasn't going to be easy as he had other offers and we were not his first choice. While the interview was scheduled for an hour, we ended up speaking for almost twice that time. At the end of the interview he said, 'Even if you pay me less, I will be joining you. If you are wondering why, it is because you made me feel valued. You knew about me even before I met you. During these two hours, it never felt like an interview, but rather like an exploratory session for a better connect. And you listened to every word I said and absorbed every detail. You encouraged me to showcase all the work I did in the past, and I was able to showcase my creativity to you, which I am proud of. This tells me I will be joining the right leader.'

I felt proud and realized that many a time, we forget that the sound of silence can be more effective than speaking out loud. Your curiosity and willingness to listen before you speak shows that you value the opinion of the other person.

His words reminded me of a coach I had a few years ago. We often took long walks during our sessions, and she allowed me to speak for almost an hour, as though she wanted me to share everything in my heart and mind before she even opened her mouth. It helped me so much to find the answers I was looking for; I learnt much from her listening ability. It is not about giving an answer to an issue instantly, it is also about exploring and letting the other person speak his or her mind.

Remaining curious and encouraging creativity is invaluable in the world we are going to face after COVID-19, with all the changes we are likely to see in the economy and society.

Apart from being open to ideas and exploring new routes to respond to a challenge, one needs to listen with all his or her attention and ask open-ended questions to clarify any ambiguity. It's a great way to show someone you care.

Demonstrate empathy

Manisha, the human resources head of an e-commerce unicorn, shared her story with me, which is a great example of what empathy can do for a great professional.

'I've had an eventful career, and I consider myself fortunate to have reached the top at an early age. Many people who deal with me know that I am a very sensitive individual, and some events that happen in the world, even if they don't directly or indirectly affect me, can send me into depression. I go into my shell when I hear about natural calamities that destroy lives. I feel tired, lose sleep, suffer from mood swings; I can't even function properly. I have tried many ways to overcome this, but I haven't been able to. When I am low, it affects my work, and I am aware of that.

'Some fail to understand why it affects me personally, while others consider me a weak personality. But what has helped is those co-workers who understand me and do their best to support me. Their messages of support and small acts of kindness are what help me recover fast. People step in to help with my work. If they had not been empathetic to my situation, I would never have reached where I am today. I am now indebted to this organization for all the support I have received.'

One can't lead from the heart without believing in empathy. Empathy is a subject by itself, one that we have touched upon in several other sections of this book. Empathy will enable us to provide psychological safety to our teams; it will allow us to lead more inclusively instead of being directional. It is no more about 'I told you so and you follow'. It is about collective wisdom that creates a safe environment that people can thrive in. Empathy also helps us deal with our own emotions, and contrary to the popular belief that we should keep emotions at bay at work, properly directed emotion can lead us to a positive outcome. Many leaders do believe that only passionate people show emotions and that those are the very same people who care about the progress of an organization. I am one of them.

It is true that emotions may lead to conflict, but that is where empathy comes into play, as leaders recognize that everyone is different and that we can deal with them all in a different style. Empathy provides the depth in professional relations and helps us stay connected beyond transactions. It helps us connect with our co-workers and get to know one another better, which in turn helps in delivery of a common objective.

Share stories

As a child, I did not like reading books, but I loved stories. As I said earlier, I looked up to the greatest storyteller I have ever met: my mother. She was always a great observer of life and could share many incidents that influenced her. She taught me life values through those stories. 'One day you will appreciate the power of storytelling, and I am sure you will use it in your life, in some way,' I remember her saying one day. 'Maybe your urge to read will develop then. Remember that you must read a book or watch a movie to enjoy yourself, but also try to take something away from the experience since you are investing a portion of your life in them. If you apply it to your life, your learning will then be a pleasure.'

We all have our dreams and aspirations. And then we face reality. Often, there are gaps between dreams and reality. Many a time, stories bridge that gap through the learning they bring to us. Hence stories are great management tools.

Let us not assume that only leaders need to share stories; in the new age, leaders will need to encourage their teams to look for stories and use them in their day-to-day lives. Stories can be captured from any medium—from life, books, movies and articles. But stories need to be relatable and believable, faking them will cause more damage than good.

The new world will look for more storytellers, rather than directive messengers and great PowerPoint presenters, as when we receive a message through a story, we know it is real and the believability quotient rises. Even better is when a story is based on personal events where a leader shows vulnerability.

Appreciate, acknowledge, show gratitude

I was talking to Lucas, a leader based in Sweden heading a diverse team across the world.

'I am always shy about appreciating others, not because I don't want to, but because it is not in me. COVID-19 made it even more difficult as I hardly met my team face-to-face, and I realized my opportunities to appreciate them and show gratitude were becoming slimmer. And that was not motivating for the team.

'My wife gave me the great idea to create a "virtual appreciation forum", a practice she has followed over the past few years with her own team. So now, every Friday evening, I hold an appreciation call where I recognize all the good work done during the week, and then I share the summary with the entire organization through our internal website. This has generated a highly engaged team.

'I can see the value of those words of praise, the bonding and motivation they create. I am not going to lose this momentum and will continue this practice even when we are back in office full time.'

Lucas has even found a way to 'fire' up this new practice. 'From an Indian friend, I heard about the Hindi word "aag", which means fire. Now I know how to create fire in my team: through A—Appreciation, A—Acknowledgement and G—Gratitude.'

Many leaders do struggle to appreciate and show gratitude when needed. In my view, everyone needs to be appreciated, even CEOs. The advantage of being face-to-face, being appreciated or acknowledged by a simple smile or pat on the back, won't exist all the time. But the need does not go away, so we must ensure we make conscious choices to show that we understand, acknowledge and appreciate each one's contribution. In the virtual world, the warmth of appreciation will need to be felt virtually.

Accept failure

Angela, a CEO based in New York, told me this story from her own experience.

'Last year I took a decision to split two businesses. In my view, they were not interlinked and the synergy I drew out of them was minimum. This impacted many of our employees and resulted in job losses. However, in hindsight, I realized I was wrong: instead of reaping benefits from the split, we ended up duplicating efforts and increasing cost. Our share prices dropped, employee dissatisfaction increased. We lost some good talent.

'I have always been known as a bold leader, and my team has looked up to me even though they are a thousand miles away. So

I stood up and admitted my mistake and decided to reverse my decision. There was a high chance of me losing my job, but I did what was right for the organization, not thinking about myself alone. My biggest learning from this debacle was to honestly stand tall. My action encouraged everyone to come forward and rework the merger. It built trust as they now know I am one of them and I can handle my vulnerability. They know I am honest and can own up to my failure.'

Leading from the heart requires leaders to learn to deal with failures. Blaming and shaming is always the easy way out, but that is not what leaders are for. We need to help our teams accept that it is okay to make mistakes and that every mistake opens up new opportunities as we learn from them. With such an open culture, we have to actively let everyone know that we believe and live by this philosophy, and that they can trust this process. We are all prone to failure and mistakes, so be vulnerable and accept it and ensure you spread positivity across the organization by looking for the opportunities at every hurdle you cross.

Treat everyone differently

This is the motto of one of the organizations I follow. It may seem to go against principles of equality and equity, but stick with me for a moment. I asked the organization's head of HR to explain the rationale behind the policy.

'Many years ago, when I was a junior manager in a manufacturing organization, I used to get angry when someone attended a meeting or discussion unprepared. I believed that he or she was wasting everyone's time, and to me, time has always been precious. I believed I was doing the right thing as I was passionate about my work. My factory head assured me that if

I was part of any meeting, everyone would attend it with due preparation. Over time, things got better.

'The day I was leaving that job, my factory head said that he had understood what had triggered my button and had ensured that it didn't happen again. From then, I've practised this trick: I try to get to know a person beyond his or her job description and really dig further to find out what kind of person he or she is, what motivates or annoys the other person, so that I can adapt myself to suit him or her better.'

Everyone is different; at the same time, everyone is alike. What I mean is that we humans all share some basic feelings such as fear, anger, hope, love, faith and disappointment, but while these are common, what triggers them differs from person to person. Knowing what triggers a button in a person, what makes him or her react in a negative way (red button), and what motivates a person to walk the extra mile (green button), will be of importance as we lead from our hearts. This simple step will give us the key to motivate or demotivate our team members, and this skill will be called upon even more as we lead from a distance.

Be emotionally resilient

Recently, Anjali, a senior finance manager working for a large global firm, told me something very interesting that touched my heart.

'It was one of those European summer months and just another Friday morning; I was expecting an easy day before my vacation. At around 11 a.m., my manager and I had a call with our Australian team. It was just a routine monthly review.

'David is the finance lead for the country, and he had Suzy and Nancy on the call with him. We started reviewing the audit progress as the deadline was nearing, and I was not confident that the team would deliver on time.

'During the discussion, David told us why he thought there might be some delays in the final closure of the audit. While David was speaking, Nancy interrupted. "You guys sitting in head office have no clue what happens on the ground. We are short of people, everyone here is working more than fourteen hours a day, the past three weekends have been spent in the office, and now you are blaming us for the delay? Why don't you come over here and complete it for us?"

'Nancy spoke in a loud tone. I thought it was quite nasty as in our organization, we don't have a culture of shouting in meetings.

'I saw my manager looking at me. He put the phone on mute and said, "Do not react, there must be more to it. Absorb the blow."

'We ended the meeting, and immediately afterwards, David called me and said, "Sorry about what happened today. Nancy should not have reacted like that."

'I replied, "Once is fine but we do not support such a culture."

'"Nancy is under a lot of stress," said David. "Apart from being overworked, she lost her dog last week and is very upset. And due to work pressure, she did not get any time to be alone and mourn."

'A few days later, Nancy called my manager. "Thanks for your understanding," she said, "your silence and support during our last review meeting taught me a lot. I remain committed and the audit will be finalized before the deadline."'

Nancy's story is not unique, but it tells us how many things can affect our mental state and as leaders, how important it is to be resilient.

Lack of face-to-face interaction, a fast pace of change, evolving technology, social media, rising unemployment, shifting employment and many other factors can create stressful situations and frustrations in ourselves and in our teams. Our personal lives are always affecting our professional lives, and we can't always segregate the two of them.

We also deal with different people coming from different cultures and backgrounds, and their degree of emotional resilience may vary as well. Emotional resilience will be a required trait as it will help us and our teams deal with such situations and adversities. As leaders, we need to ensure we help our team members deal with difficult situations with empathy, trying to understand why someone is behaving a certain way, and being aware of their state of mind, listening to them and supporting them by coaching and mentoring with optimism and positivity.

Develop people as a passion

Recently, Ashok, a senior manager based in Ahmedabad, told me about a conversation he had with his CFO during his annual appraisal meeting.

'Someone took the pain to develop me and hence I am here. Now it is my turn to do the same for you and this is my way of giving back to my organization in the form of the next CFO. Till now, I developed people as a hobby, but this should have been my passion. The new age will see rapid change, a much faster pace of change than in the past, and everyone needs to develop themselves and develop their teams every day to cope with it all and remain relevant. You can't treat developing people as a hobby like I did; let this be your passion. And this will be my passion as well from today onwards. Better late than never.'

We spoke earlier in the book about how the next phase of the corporate world will experience a lot of unlearning and relearning. We need to accept that there will be a gap in our skill set, be it in technical matters or in our ways of working, and we need to develop ourselves to bridge these gaps. The same will hold true for our teams. Developing people will not be an option anymore, but a compulsion for our leaders.

Be a coach and a mentor

During my coach training programme, I met Jack, a retired army officer. He had tons of energy, and being a war veteran, had many stories to share. I was a good student, always eager to listen to his stories. One day Jack told me about how his experience of civilian life hadn't always been so smooth.

'My life stories are of interest to many civilians as they have not experienced my world. I have gone through much, risked my life many times and have never been scared. And then one day, I retired and joined the corporate world as a confident man. But that very day, my worries began as I realized how naïve I had been about my new environment. In no time, I went into depression, and finally I appointed a coach to help me. That helped boost my confidence.

'Then one day, I met a bunch of youngsters at our cafeteria, and I started mingling with them. I realized that I may have enough life experience, but their world was so different—the way they thought, the way they solved problems, the way they planned, the knowledge they had. They knew my background and were interested to know about my experiences and hear my war stories. I agreed to share with them if they would mentor me in turn. At first they laughed it off, but then they finally agreed. That process helped me so much, and today I stand here confidently because I took that step.'

I believe everyone needs to be coached and mentored at some point of time. It is not only senior leaders who need to coach their juniors, it can be vice versa based on need, just as we saw in Jack's story. This might not yet be common practice, but we can expect it to become more popular as the need grows.

We have spoken about how distance working will require us to handle others' emotions with greater care. This will give rise to the need for more coaching and mentoring in the corporate world, as we will all need such guidance and help, even if it is just someone to listen to our challenges and understand us. Even senior leaders need to be open to reverse mentoring, so that they might learn from younger talent or those with different skills. We can't be shy about seeking such interventions or providing them as we lead from our hearts, else we will deny ourselves the opportunity for continuous learning.

Let go

A few months ago I was chatting with Sangyu, the quality head of a consumer durables company based in Shanghai, about a problem he had encountered.

'We have many plants across the country, and I have defined clear processes to ensure we have the same quality standards across all manufacturing facilities. I am a quality freak and I do not allow anyone to bypass my instructions. Whatever people choose to say about me—good or bad—I have never cared. I have only been concerned about my organizational reputation and my customers.

'Over the last few years, I noticed that most customer returns were machines manufactured in one plant. I travelled there many times, reviewed their processes but could not determine the root cause. A few months ago, a new quality engineer joined, and from then on I noticed that customer returns from that plant came down drastically.

'Upon a deep dive, I realized that he had put in a few new processes that were not defined by me. I was not happy, and when I asked why they had violated the global process, I was told that a particular component had been failing to perform, which was causing the machine to fail. The component, sourced from a local supplier, needed a bit of calibration at our end. Since the process I had defined did not have that step, no one before had dared to take that deviation. Everyone had followed the process blindly.

'The new engineer had the courage to deviate and solve the issue. To be honest, I had to swallow my ego, but this showed me I needed to let go and delegate more power to my team, rather than keep it to myself in these days of agile working. That doesn't mean they can deviate from global processes, but they can tweak as needed without me being involved at every level.'

Remote working calls for delegation with accountability clearly defined. Fixing clear responsibilities and accountabilities is the key to success in such a working atmosphere. Gone are the days when decisions were taken at the top and everyone else only executed orders. In the technology-enabled new world, the need for delegation is even more important, and that means leaders need to create empowered teams that can decide and act within the agreed-upon framework to facilitate quicker decision-making. This also means that people need to take ownership of their areas of control and deliver as needed.

Celebrate and have fun

Sahana is the quality manager for a car accessory manufacturer based in Gurgaon. Her team figured out a way to celebrate success even during these times of social distancing.

'As an organization, we were always shy to declare an accomplishment as a success, since we worried about sustaining the same level of performance. So, many a time, even outstanding results were not celebrated, which caused dissatisfaction amongst our employees. COVID-19 taught us how vulnerable we are as human beings and how uncertain the world can become in a day. We all know most industries have struggled to keep up through the pandemic, and we were no different. The situation was becoming more and more depressing with every passing week.

'Then one day we, as a team, got together and decided to celebrate every little success or achievement. I think that was the best decision we have taken in many years. Now, every Thursday evening, we gather over a video call and cheer every achievement of that week. The mood of the team has completely changed. We realized celebration is not an annual event over a gala dinner; it can be a simple virtual pat on the back, and needs to be done often. Now I look forward to the next Thursday. People now know we are an organization that knows how to celebrate, that cares and has a big heart.'

The corporate world is shy about celebrating success or having fun. Celebrating the small things does not come naturally to many organizations. Many leaders feel that celebrations should happen for big achievements, and thus they are often about the team hitting the pub together or going out for dinner. Indeed, that is a nice way to celebrate, but I always argue that celebration is never restricted to good food and wine. Celebration is about recognizing a good effort or a good outcome, and simply talking about it. It does not have to be linked to something big. This can be done with a few words of appreciation, claps, notes, a virtual pat on the back, a simple smile, or some other innovative method. Having fun does not have a fixed formula;

different people will have different ways to celebrate, hence let us not restrict ourselves to one single formula. With the ways of working changing, we will be physically separated from each other for some time to come and celebrating under the same roof may not always be possible. So why wait to have fun?

Take care

Aruna, an HR manager based in Mumbai, told me a beautiful story.

'I read about virtual fatigue in one of your articles, but I never believed in it. For me, during COVID-19, nothing changed except that I was working remotely from my home office. I was still talking to my colleagues every day, doing all my tasks. In fact, initially I felt I had more time than ever. But then, after a few months, I started feeling tired, the days seemed to be longer than ever, it was never-ending! I was not delivering on my commitments on time, my quality of work suffered and finally I felt claustrophobic in my own house—the very house that I loved so much!

'I was not sure what was happening to me, so I read your article again but still did not believe I was suffering from virtual fatigue. I told my manager about my state of mind, and from that day, he called me every morning as he started his day, and every evening as he finished his day, to ensure that I was not overworked or feeling alone. He helped me plan my priorities and ensured that I took up only what I could deliver. In a few weeks, I stared performing again and regaining my confidence. He truly showed me that a little care can save someone from being burnt out; he taught me what leading from the heart means.'

Limited face-to-face interactions coupled with process-based models and technological advances may give some people the sense that they are being taken over by technology, or are alone, or are not being included, which can lead to stress and burnout. This is where understanding one another, communicating heart-to-heart beyond the regular nine-to-five job becomes helpful, and a new-age leader needs to handle all such situations with care to ensure virtual fatigue is held at bay, or to proactively take steps to address cases of fatigue that have already set it. A tired body or a tired mind can't continue to lead from the front with agility.

Conclusion

I started this book by saying that we need to adapt, evolve and shine or we can decide to wait, watch and perish. It is our life, our career, our choice, but the world is not going to wait for any of us.

We also started the book with five pertinent questions:

1. Do I have the skills required in this changing world?
2. Will I survive in this fast-changing world?
3. Will my team be valued for the skills they have today, or do they need something else?
4. How do we prepare the next generation for a workplace that we haven't even begun to imagine?
5. If the biggest changes are thanks to technology and the evolving ways of working in a purpose-driven world, what

can we do to ensure that we stay relevant in the years to come?

I hope you now have a clearer understanding of the needs of this world that we must all adapt to, and how we can do so. Hopefully this knowledge and awareness will steer us to the next stage in this fast-changing world, and our journey will be purpose-led, digitally-enabled and virtually-driven.

As I have said before, this book does not contain a secret formula to overcome all uncertainty in your career. But it aims to help you navigate it with greater awareness, lots of preparation and most importantly, by identifying the core traits you need to grow and develop to make yourself future-proof.

If I have been slightly preachy at times, it was to stress a point. As professionals, I am confident you will understand the spirit in which it was meant.

As you return to your regular routine, please take some time out to sit back and think about the stories you read here. Then critically introspect about the gaps in your own skill set and the traits you need to develop and adapt to be the kind of leader the corporate world needs in the coming decades. While you might feel that many of these issues do not affect your career or life at the moment, don't be surprised if they hit you sooner than you expect. So why not act right now and get ahead of the game?

Let us start opening our minds to embrace the changes, start leading through our hearts, through processes and through technology. Once we have made these part of our value system, we should be able to meet the challenges of today and tomorrow with resilience and power.

Let us outskill. Let us begin.

'To begin, begin'.

—*William Wordsworth*

Leaders Who Contributed

All opinions/statements expressed by the leaders or by me are purely personal and have no relevance to their/ my past or present employer/s or any other associations. All stories are fictional and any resemblance to any person, living or dead, is purely coincidental.

The designations of some leaders may have changed in the time since they contributed to this book and it was published.

Human resources leaders

- Anushree Singh, Country Human Resources Director, India subcontinent, AkzoNobel
- Dr P.V. Ramana Murthy, Executive Vice President and Global Head, Human Resources, Taj Hotels
- Himal Tiwari, Chief Human Resources Officer, Tata Power Ltd

- Prriti Narain, Human Resources Lead, GBO Sales, Google, USA
- Surajit Banerjee, Senior Vice President and Head, Human Resources, SpiceJet Ltd

Finance leaders

- Dilip Pal, Chief Financial Officer, Safaricom PLC
- Jayesh Desai, former Head of Investment, Piramal Enterprises Ltd
- Kiran Koteshwar, Chief Financial Officer, SpiceJet Ltd
- Manish Gupta, Senior Vice President and Chief Financial Officer, Member of Board, Mitsubishi Mahindra Agricultural Machinery Co. Ltd
- Naveen Begwani, Vice President and Controller, EMEA, Kohler Co.
- Ramanan G.V., Vice President Finance and Group Controller, Tata Motors Ltd
- Sameer Agarwal, Chief Financial Officer, Manipal Health Enterprises Pvt. Ltd
- Sandeep Batra, Chief Financial Officer, Crompton Greaves Consumer Electricals
- Sunil Gupta, Chief Financial Officer, Bottling Investments Group, The Coca-Cola Company

Functional/business leaders

- Arunabha Ghosh, Head, Oracle Presales, EAS (Europe), Tata Consultancy Services
- Deepa Dey, Head, Communication and Sustainability, Nutrition and Special Projects, Hindustan Unilever Limited
- Dhiren Kinger, Associate Director, KPMG Global Services

- Diptendu Mondal, Director Sourcing, Ericsson
- Monideepa Bhattacharya, Director, Business Development, BRIDGEi2i Analytics Solutions
- Pranesh Chatterjee, Manager Technology, Projects and Strategy, Tata Steel Europe
- Sarmila Basu, Senior Director, Data and Decision Sciences, Microsoft
- Subroto Gupta, Chief Innovation and Transformation Officer, Compass Group

Chief information/technical officers

- Ashok Cherian, Chief Information Officer, Page Industries, former chief information officer Emami Agrotech, JK Cement
- Anil Nashier, Chief Technology Officer, COFRA Holding A.G.
- Rajesh Dangi, Chief Technical Officer, NxtGen Infinite Datacenter
- Subodh Dubey, Global Chief Information Officer, Suzlon Group
- Suman Ghose, author, *From Command to Empathy*, former Lead—Information System, Philips Electronics India Ltd

Chief executive officers/partners

- Arunabh Das Sharma, former President, Bennett Coleman and Co. Ltd
- Ashish Aul, Partner, KPMG India
- Gopi Koteeswaran, Chief Executive Officer, LatentView
- Haresh Hemrajani, Managing Director, Head of Banking, Card and Enterprise Payments Solutions Presales, UK/Europe, FIS
- Indraneel Roy Choudhury, Partner, PWC India

- Manish Bhatia, Managing Director and Chief Executive Officer, DIC India Ltd
- Nikhil Dey, Executive Director, Adfactors PR
- Puneet Gupta, Managing Director, Franke Faber India Ltd
- Prabal Mitra, Managing Director, Accenture, Netherlands
- Ravi Sahgal, Executive Vice President and Business Head, Kurlon Limited
- Sanjesh Thakur, Partner, Deloitte India
- Satyakam Basu, External Advisor, Bain and Company
- Shridhar Narayan, Group Director and Chief Executive Officer—Infrastructure (Industrial and Logistics), Hiranandani Group
- Shyam Mamidi, former Partner and Vice President, IBM
- Soumen Mukherjee, Partner, CFO Services, Deloitte Netherlands
- Sreenivasa Rao Yadavilli, former Managing Director India, Korn Ferry Futurestep
- Syed Safawi, former Managing Director and Group Chief Executive Officer, VLCC
- Vineet Kumar Kapila, Global Head, Main Stream Spirits, Diageo

Acknowledgements

I would like to convey my sincere thanks and gratitude to all the leaders who provided me with their valuable comments and participated in various discussions to help me shape this book. In a true sense, they are my co-authors.

I would also like to thank my corporate colleagues, many of whom will probably never realize how they have contributed to this book. Through their journeys, they imparted invaluable knowledge to me, which found its way into this book.

My readers and friends for their encouragement through numerous emails, Facebook, LinkedIn, Instagram and personal messages.

Krishan Chopra, former publisher at HarperCollins Publishers India, for his caring attitude and encouragement at every stage of my interaction.

Sachin Sharma, Executive Editor, HarperCollins Publishers India, for coming up with the title of this book, his continuous involvement and clear guidance. Without his encouragement, this book would not have taken the shape that it has today. Though I live miles away from India, I never felt the distance, thanks to his support.

Madhumita Bhattacharyya for her help with research and initial editing during the writing of the book.

Sumit Dasgupta, Founder, ALLCAP Communications, for helping me shape my thoughts and for introducing me to Madhumita.

Adreja Mukherji for helping me interview a few of the leaders and compiling their thoughts.

Alessandro Punturo, my coach, for constantly encouraging me to finish the book.

Sayanti, my wife, for her critical comments, and for her idea to include 'near-life stories' in the book, and my children Rayan and Anavi for constantly encouraging me.

And lastly, I request forgiveness of all those who have supported me during this journey, but whose names I have failed to mention.

About the Author

Partha Basu brings in his years of research on the future of leadership, his keen observation power, storytelling and people skills to this book.

He has worked for international/Indian companies, lived in India and abroad, which has immensely helped him shape up his leadership thoughts over years.

In the last 30 years, Partha has work in seven industries, both in Fortune 500 organizations like Coca-Cola, Whirlpool, AkzoNobel, Tata Group as well in new initiatives like IFB-Bosch and SpiceJet.

Partha has earlier authored five books—*Lifescapes: The Long and Short of It* (2021), *Mid-career Crisis* (2015), *Make It or Break It* (2012), *With or Without You* (2010) and *Why Not!* (2008). He has delivered lectures in India and abroad and his articles have been published widely.

Presently, he is based out of Amsterdam, Netherlands.

30 Years *of*

 HarperCollins *Publishers* India

At HarperCollins, we believe in telling the best stories and finding the widest possible readership for our books in every format possible. We started publishing 30 years ago; a great deal has changed since then, but what has remained constant is the passion with which our authors write their books, the love with which readers receive them, and the sheer joy and excitement that we as publishers feel in being a part of the publishing process.

Over the years, we've had the pleasure of publishing some of the finest writing from the subcontinent and around the world, and some of the biggest bestsellers in India's publishing history. Our books and authors have won a phenomenal range of awards, and we ourselves have been named Publisher of the Year the greatest number of times. But nothing has meant more to us than the fact that millions of people have read the books we published, and somewhere, a book of ours might have made a difference.

As we step into our fourth decade, we go back to that one word – a word which has been a driving force for us all these years.

Read.

Harper
Collins

HARPER
PERENNIAL

HARPER
BUSINESS

HARPER
BLACK

हार्पर
हिन्दी

HarperCollins
Children'sBooks

HARPER
DESIGN

HARPER
VANTAGE

Harper
Sport